The Family and the New Right

Pamela Abbott and Claire Wallace

Foreword by Robert Moore

PLUTO PRESS

LONDON • BOULDER, COLORADO

First published 1992 by Pluto Press
345 Archway Road, London N6 5AA
and 5500 Central Avenue, Boulder, Colorado, USA

Copyright © Pamela Abbott and Claire Wallace 1992
Foreword copyright © Robert Moore 1992

British Library Cataloguing in Publication Data
A catalogue record for this book is available from the British Library

ISBN 0 7453 05326 hbk
ISBN 0 7453 05334 pbk

Library of Congress Cataloging-in-Publication Data
Abbott, Pamela.
    The family and the new right / Pamela Abbott and Claire Wallace
        p. cm. – (Pluto perspectives)
    Includes bibliographical references and index
    ISBN 0-7453-0532-6 (hb). –ISBN 0-7453-0533-4 (pb)
    1. Family–Great Britain. 2. Family–United States. 3. Family
policy–Great Britain. 4. Family policy–United States.
5. Conservatism–Great Britain. 6. Conservatism–United States.
I. Wallace, Claire. II. Title. III. Series
HQ614.A23 1992
306.85'0941–dc20
                                                                    92-4668
                                                                        CIP

Typeset from authors' disks by
Stanford Desktop Publishing Services, Milton Keynes
Printed in Finland by WSOY

The Family and the New Right

PLUTO PERSPECTIVES

Series Editor Professor Robert Moore

Pluto Perspectives has created a forum for independent academics and commentators to offer sustained analytical critiques of individuals, institutions, themes and movements on what has now come to be identified as the 'New Right'.

Already published:

The New Crusaders:
Christianity and the New Right
in Southern Africa
PAUL GIFFORD

Citizenship and Social Class
T. H. MARSHALL and TOM BOTTOMORE

Hayek and the Market
JIM TOMLINSON

Forthcoming title:

Philosophy and the New Right
TED BENTON

Dr Pamela Abbott is Principal Lecturer in Sociology and Social Policy at the University of Plymouth. Publications include: *Women and Social Class* (with Roger Sapsford, 1987), *An Introduction to Sociology: Feminist Perspectives* (with Claire Wallace, 1990); *The Sociology of the Caring Professions* (with Claire Wallace, 1990); *Gender, Power and Sexuality* (with Claire Wallace, 1991), and *Research Methods for Nurses and the Caring Professions* (with Roger Sapsford, 1992).

Claire Wallace is lecturer in Applied Social Science, Lancaster University, presently on secondment to the European University in Prague. Publications include: *For Richer, For Poorer: Growing Up In and Out of Work* (1987); *Lives of their Own* (with G. Jones, 1992); and several titles co-authored with Pamela Abbott (see above).

Robert Moore is Professor of Sociology at the University of Liverpool and a distinguished author.

To Harvey and Santana,
with whom we spent many happy hours
riding on Dartmoor
while discussing the ideas for this book

Contents

Foreword

Robert Moore

This present volume is the latest in the 'Pluto Perspective' series, which aims to introduce students to the ideas of the New Right as they have emerged mainly in the United States and Europe in recent years. Debates on the family, and the position of women within the family, have been particularly intense in the United States, and the work of the American theorists and writers features strongly in this book.

The debates range over issues from women's ownership and control of property to the ownership and control of their own bodies. These concerns are hardly new: they have been the subject of discussion for over a century. And it appears that the changing position of women in society is inevitably linked – by the Right – to a perception of society in 'decline', as demonstrated in the following pages. The status of women and the state of the family in general are seen to be a litmus test for the state of society.

As we approach the twenty-first century, there are few new interests in the conflicts, though new arguments are sometimes introduced to defend old positions. Yet while the medical and biological reasoning of the latter part of the nineteenth century now strike us as risible, and we may marvel at the gullibility of our forebears, the authors of this book, sociologists Pamela Abbott and Claire Wallace, have plainly encountered modern authors whom they find hard to read with a straight face. Yet these are authors whose influence is sufficient for us to be forced to take them seriously, and it is for this reason that their work is discussed in this volume.

When authors are not taken seriously in their own country they will sometimes seek to spread their ideas abroad. Though they may become figures of fun, subjected to the ridicule of those who move in academic circles, from time to time their ideas find a wide currency in the world of politics. This is a hazard against which Abbott and Wallace's work is a timely warning. The main criticisms of George Gilder and Charles Murray, whose work is discussed in this book, is that they have little credible evidence to sustain their theories. Furthermore their theories have served an all too obvious function in the retreat from welfare and the creation of a harsher and less caring society in the US. The authors are deeply anti-egalitarian, and Murray at least would seek to uncouple private deprivation from the effects of public policy. Their work seems therefore to be more ideological than scholarly.

Whatever their intellectual merits, however, the ideas of Gilder and Murray have crossed the Atlantic from the US to Europe. Conduits have been provided by right-wing think tanks, pressure groups and 'concerned businessmen'. Murray's work was described by Kenneth Baker when he was Britain's Minister of Education as 'brilliant'. It is important therefore that we understand these ideas, their origins and implications and perhaps, most importantly, the interests they serve. These are important in explaining the appeal of ideas that might seem to lack a firm basis in evidence. The ideas of Gilder and Murray are travelling far and are now finding a ready audience in Eastern Europe where they enable converts to market theories to account for unemployment, poverty and family dislocation without having to implicate the market itself.

Paradoxically Gilder's arguments for getting women back into the home depend upon a view of men as debased animals who need the ministrations of women to civilise them. Ideas such as these may be found in work written on training women for their domestic duties at the turn of the century. There is little new about the ideas. The interesting question is why they so persistently return when evidence to support them has been entirely lacking in every historical manifestation. The boundary between scholarship and belief in such a contended terrain is easily blurred. But the ease with which the boundary may be crossed makes it an important one to study.

One striking feature of the new right is the extent to which it has not engaged with its critics, but simply seeks to dismiss or discredit them. The most common reply to criticism is to suggest that the left are seeking to mount a show trial and that the terms of the debate are rigged. This series and this volume introduce new right ideas in a critical way. The authors make no pretence of adopting a dispassionate stance but, having engaged the reader, invite him or her to explore further by providing an ample bibliography.

The ideas of the new right writers on the family and the status of women appeal to old prejudices – and they do so in times of change and crisis. As Abbott and Wallace show, there have been changes in family life, derived from demographic, economic and political developments. The social changes interact with the demands of women, which have a history as long as those which would deny them. The demands become part of the social changes; they shape one another. The person caught up in and perplexed by change finds it hard to understand how world historical trends intersect his or her biography. In such situations theories that stress the personal and the individual at the expense of the institutional have a powerful attraction. Similarly appeals to common sense exert a strong influence at exactly those times when received wisdom provides no means to understand change.

Robert Moore
August 1992

Introduction

The 'New Right' has been a topic of much discussion and debate over the last ten years and there are many books explaining and analysing its philosophies and policies. The policies have served to attack welfare spending, to attack feminism and 'permissive' notions of the family and to strengthen 'law and order'. Although neither Reagan nor Thatcher is still in office, the ideas and policies which they supported have shaped the economic, social and intellectual climate of the late twentieth century. The administrations headed by Margaret Thatcher in the UK and Ronald Reagan in the US were seen as heavily influenced by New Right economic, political and moral ideas. The extent to which they were successful in implementing New Right policies – or even the consistency with which they coherently followed New Right ideas – is disputed. Indeed, arguably, different elements of New Right thinking are contradictory – the New Right is made up of a number of strands which do not necessarily integrate into a coherent ideology. Nevertheless, Thatcherism and Reaganism were influenced by the ideas of what is generally referred to as the New Right. While the political systems in which they operated were different – a unitary one in the UK and a federal one in the US – and the precise policies they advocated were not identical, they both combined a commitment to liberal economic policies with support for conservative social and moral values. That is, they both advocated free markets, low direct taxation and limited government regulation of industry. Rejecting Keynesian demand-managed economic policies, they advocated reduced government spending, especially on welfare programmes, but argued for high defence spending. Both gave vocal support to social and moral movements of the Right, stressing individual responsibility and the primacy of Christian moral values.

Nearly all of the academic discussion has focused upon economic liberalism and its influence upon the social and economic policies of Margaret Thatcher in Britain and Ronald Reagan in the US. However, central to New Right philosophy is a set of assumptions about the family and about relationships between men and women. As Paul Johnson (a British New Right journalist and intellectual) has said, the family is a central prop to the New Right vision of the world: 'The ideal society must rest upon the tripod of a strong family, a voluntary church and a liberal minimal state. Of these, the family is the most important' (Johnson, 1982). Yet gender and the family are seldom discussed and get no mention in most of the commentaries on the New Right. We intend to redress this omission in this book by focusing upon the New Right's family discourse.

The group within the New Right which engages in this discourse is generally referred to as the *Moral* Right, a collection of pressure groups including Christian and pro-family campaigning groups. There are also a number of influential intellectuals on both sides of the Atlantic who have provided a coherent and theoretically informed basis for the moral and familial arguments of the New Right. Indeed, from their analysis of social and economic trends some of these maintain that Britain's and America's social problems are caused not so much by the failure of economic policies as by moral decline (Davies, 1987). Ronald Reagan in the United States and Margaret Thatcher in Britain both pledged allegiance to the familial and moral as well as to the economic arguments of the New Right.

In this book we shall address the Moral Right and their ideas about gender relations and the family. We argue that an under-standing of these is essential both for making sense of the New Right and for understanding how different and contradictory strands of economic liberalism and traditional conservatism articulate together in current political discourse. It is also essential for under-standing why rolling back the state – including welfare – is seen as a way to solve economic and social problems. The family is the lynchpin of New Right economic and social policies because within this discourse men are seen as the 'individuals' of economic liberal thought while women are seen as outside the market place, a part of the dependent family, not citizens in their own right (Abbott and Wallace, 1989). The British Conservative Party Conference in 1990 yet again focused on the family and family issues and restated the position that while families need to stand on their own feet and take responsibility for their members, it is up to the state to make sure that they do so. Furthermore, the Conservative Party was once more set up as the one to defend the good and wholesome family from those who would bring it down: 'The enemies of the Conservative Party are the enemies of the family – socialists who have brought together and politicised every deviant minority opposed to family life and, almost worse, Liberals' (Adrian Rogers, at the Conservative Party Conference, 1990).

We start by examining ideologies of the family and the relation-ship between welfarism and familialism. We then examine the rise of the 'moral' New Right both in the US and in Britain and appraise the work of some of the leading and most influential New Right intel-lectuals. Their ideas have helped to shape the ideological climate which made Thatcherism and Reaganism a possibility prior to their coming to power, and they have since provided texts and articles which give coherence to an otherwise shifting and *ad hoc* set of policies. Their influence is pervasive throughout Britain, the US, Canada and Australia because of the circulation of written texts in English between these countries and because of the various 'think tanks' and privately-funded policy institutes around which intellectuals circulate (see Taylor, 1990). These were set up to develop economic and social policies for the New Right and had close links both with each other and with the cabinets of Mrs Thatcher and Mr Reagan. Examples include: the Adam Smith Institute, originally founded in the US in 1978 and in Britain in 1981; the Centre for Policy Studies set up in Britain in 1974 by Margaret Thatcher and Keith Joseph; and the Institute of Economic Affairs, also in Britain, founded in 1956. The Adam Smith Institute in particular has close links with the Heritage Foundation, a very large privately-funded policy studies institute in the US, established in 1974 (see *Labour Research* 1984, 1985 and 1989).

We have selected for particular attention the work of Roger Scruton and Ferdinand Mount in Britain, and from the US George Gilder, Martin Anderson, Lawrence Mead and Charles Murray. A critical appraisal of the ideas of these authors needs to be set in the context of the social movements underlying the Moral Right – the Christian, anti-abortion and pro-family movements. These movements have been more influential in the United States than in Great Britain. In the United States their influence has spread through the traditional popularity of revivalist and charismatic Christianity and been given additional publicity through television and radio, and they were mobilised as a political force during the 1970s and 1980s. However, a more moderate Christian Right also exists within Britain and has strong links with the Conservative Party.

Next we examine the social policies developed under 'Thatcherism' and 'Reaganism' during the 1980s in the light of the way in which they have been influenced by ideologies of gender, the family and morality. While neither the United States nor Britain has an explicit family policy, families and family life are profoundly influenced by social and economic policies, and any evaluation of the influence of the New Right must be concerned with how its policies have actually been experienced by families. It seems to us essential to understand their reasoning, since policies based on their recommendations have shaped the debates and the possibilities for setting up alternatives in the 1990s and into the twenty-first century. Indeed, we shall go further and argue that the ideas of the 'pro-family' movement have come to dominate the agenda in discussions of the family. We conclude by arguing that we need to go beyond critical evaluation of New Right ideas and to develop an alternative view of how men, women and children can relate to each other, and of the role of the state in supporting and sustaining the social citizenship of all.

1
Familialism in New Right Thinking

In 1983 Berger and Berger published a book entitled *The War over the Family*, describing the battle that was taking place in the United States between feminists and the Christian New Right over the definition of the family. This signalled the extent to which the family and family life had become a focal point of public political debate. The situation was similar in Britain, with both the Labour and Conservative parties during the 1979 general election campaign arguing that they were the 'Party of the Family'. What was new about this was not that concern was being expressed about family life nor that it was considered political, but the form which these debates took. It was evident that there was no longer (if there ever had been) a consensus on what was meant by the term 'the family', nor on what government policies best served the family's interests (and by implication the interests of society more generally).

Arguments that the family was in decline were not new. For example, in the 1950s and 1960s there had been concern about rising divorce rates, pre-marital sex and 'latchkey' children. What was new in the 1980s was the explicit attack on women who were seen as stepping outside their roles as defined by the traditional patriarchal family; especially criticised were feminists, who were seen as causing or exacerbating the patriarchal family's disintegration by challenging the male role as family head. What was also new was the ways in which these arguments articulated with the ideas of the 'economic New Right' to explain the causes of and suggest solutions for the economic crisis of the 1970s. By 1980 both Britain and the United States had administrations that were – or claimed to be – committed to the ideas of the economic and moral New Right. The arguments of the moral New Right came to take the centre of the stage in the 1980s and to a large extent have set the current agenda for discussions on the family, family policy and morality, as well as playing a key role in debates over welfare spending. They have successfully reinstated the patriarchal, self-reliant nuclear family as being the norm. Those who hold any alternative view have been put on the defensive. As Carol Smart (1984) has pointed out, the New Right's image of the family and women's role in it has popular appeal because it presents a picture of how many people want to construct their private lives – an image of Mum, Dad and the kids happily living together with

5

why image is appealing

the children growing up as well-educated, law-abiding citizens in a secure environment.

The moral New Right were reacting against what is often portrayed as the permissive sexual climate of the 1960s; against permissive parenthood (which is seen as leading to disturbed and uncontrollable children); against the 'breakdown' of the traditional family through rising divorce and illegitimacy rates; against state income maintenance programmes which take away from parents the responsibility of providing for their children; against the power of welfare professionals who take control of children away from parents; and especially against women's and gay people's rights. They attacked what they saw as a society in which women put their own needs before the needs of others (particularly the needs of their husbands). All this, they argued, had led to a self-perpetuating cycle of breakdown in the moral authority of the family – particularly the authority of the father. They conclude that this has in turn led to increasing dependency on the welfare state and an attitude of expecting the state to provide rather than providing for oneself and one's family. Welfarism and the breakdown of familial responsibility are seen as the cause of rises in juvenile delinquency, crime, illiteracy and school drop-out rates, unemployment, the spread of AIDS and growth in the numbers of people dependent on state benefits.

The appeal of the New Right is one of nostalgia – for a lost past when children respected parents, the crime rate was low, marriage was for life and the streets were safe for everyone to walk in. What is concealed when this image of the past is invoked is that it was never a reality but an ideal, a middle-class dream. It ignores not only the high crime rates of, say, Victorian London (where there were 'no-go areas' even for the police), the Victorian sexual double standard (whereby women were expected to be faithful but men could consort with prostitutes and have affairs), the physical abuse of women and children in the domestic sphere, and the economic dispossession of women which forced them either into dependence upon the family or into destitution outside it. It also ignores the appalling conditions under which working-class men, women and children sold their labour, the hardship in the absence of state pensions, disability and sickness assistance and help for the unemployed, and the real poverty and pauperisation of a significant section of the population, who were simply unable to provide for themselves. (See, for example, Steadman Jones, 1971.) Indeed, so-called Victorian 'morality' sanctioned the conditions which led to cholera, typhoid, starvation, prostitution and child labour. The lost society is not a 'golden age' but one that secured the interests of capitalism and patriarchy at the expense of the working class, of women and of children. Indeed, this is what many in the New Right would appear to want to re-create: a society

in which women are subservient to men, and the restoration of
free-market capitalism in which working-class men and some women
are forced into low-paid work, often in dirty and dangerous conditions.
What is threatened, therefore, is not the stability of the nation but
the middle-class man's stable, organised system of privilege and
prestige. As Rosalind Petchesky (1984) has put it:

> The aim of the 'pro-family' movement is to restore heterosexual
> patriarchy, the control of men over their wives and children. Teenage
> sexuality, homosexuality, the freely determined sexuality of women as
> wives and daughters, abortion, contraception, insofar as they promote
> sexual freedom, even 'test-tube' babies which hold out the prospect
> of totally removing procreation from heterosexual monogamy – all are
> a direct threat to male authority and the identification of men as
> heads of families. Given this, it is not surprising that all these activities
> have become the central target of a movement that is led by middle-
> class conservative men. The men of the 'pro-family' movement, mainly
> upper middle-class professionals, are not immune to the sense of
> personal loss that is provoked by feminism and by recent changes in
> the family and women's work. Weyrich ... captures the sense of this
> middle-class patriarchal resentment when he proclaims, 'The Father's
> word has to prevail.' (Petchesky, 1984, p. 232)

Morality, the New Right and the Family

The moral New Right stress the *moral* decay of society. Nevertheless,
there is a clear relationship between moral and economic decline.

> History confirms that the connection between declining morality and
> national decline is not just fanciful; the Roman Empire declined not just
> because of immorality and personal license but because of the
> burdensome taxation and state superstructure which the former had
> made necessary. There followed centuries during which civilisation
> regressed and it was largely the spread of Christianity which provided
> not only a moral basis to society but which indeed protected indi-
> viduals and became the stimulus for enterprise. Today we forget at our
> peril that it is the Judeo-Christian teaching, on which our personal
> behaviour has been fashioned, which is the moral basis of our society.
> (Rogers and Clements, 1985, p. 5)

There is a clear mutual reinforcement of social and economic
ideologies in the moral New Right; economic and moral decline are
not just happening at the same time – the latter is causing the
former. To stem the economic decline of capitalist countries it is
essential to re-moralise them.

I speak from my heart as well as my head. I personally deeply believe that our economic wars, our military wars and our political wars are not really our wars. These are not our problems. They are the result of our problem. Our problem is a moral, spiritual problem. All of these others are a result of that problem, and so therefore I am 180 degrees positioned against those who say that the only thing to handle is the economic problem. (Ed McAteer, founder of the New Right organisation the Religious Roundtable, quoted in Klatch, 1987, p. 28)

The moral decline of society is seen partly as the result of secularisation (a decline in the influence of Judeo-Christian values), but also an outcome of state intervention in the private sphere. Legislation is seen as undermining the heterosexual, patriarchal nuclear family and suggesting that alternative ways of living are equally acceptable. Parental control over their children's moral and religious education is said to have been undermined by, for example, sex education in schools. The family itself has been undermined by legislation for abortion and easier divorce. Husbands' control over their wives has been reduced by equal opportunities legislation and the granting of welfare benefits to unmarried and divorced mothers. Alternative life-styles are actually encouraged by the legalisation of homosexuality and the payment of welfare to single-parent families. Finally, the welfare state itself undermines the role of the family, and especially the male bread-winner's role in providing for its members. Central to this, however, is the view that the importance of the family has declined – that people are concerned about themselves and their own lives rather than for the welfare of their family and community and that individuals are no longer 'active citizens'. This, we shall see, comes out clearly in the writings of the intellectual New Right described in Chapters 4 and 5, who see men and women as no longer putting nation and family first. One American woman active in a local pro-family group in the United States told Rebecca Klatch:

I think our society is in decay. Everyone is so concerned about themselves, the 'me' generation ... But this is the time to stay close to home to protect the family in these times of trouble. There are too many humanists running around. All these people jogging and so concerned about themselves ... You have mothers who want to go out and have a career, children who know their parents don't have time for them so they turn to other kids for advice, and husbands who think it is okay for them to have extra-curricular activities. The family is falling apart. (Klatch, 1987, pp. 26–7)

According to the moral New Right, not only does the family discipline men and women in economic and sexual terms, but it also socialises children (see Chapter 5). The properly functioning family instils in children the 'correct' moral values, the core values of society. Thus the morality of the family restrains human passions and self-interest; the family provides the moral basis for the moral society. The breakdown of the family is the cause of moral decay in society and is brought about by the growth of the state and state intervention both in the private sphere and in the economy. State intervention hastens the breakdown of the family, by 'enabling' divorce and providing welfare payments for single-parent families, and is 'forced' to intervene because of the moral decay of society. People come to rely on the state rather than on their own initiative, and this growth of the state endangers individual freedom and stifles individual initiative. It takes away people's ability to control their own lives and pays for this by imposing a high tax burden on citizens and on business, which in turn stifles the entrepreneurial spirit:

> We should support the family as an institution. The family is a real alternative to the state, in fact a force for individual freedom and the first-line safety net for the welfare of the individual. It provides a bulwark against the encroachment of the state on the individual. Indeed, the quality of our citizenship is determined by the quality of our family life, and it is through the caring authority of parents that individuals learn to be independent. (Rogers and Clements, 1985, p. 56; see also Mount in Chapter 4)

Central to the moral decay of society is a breakdown in family life and in the family taking on responsibility for the economic support of its members and for their morality. The breakdown of the family – as evidenced by working mothers (who by taking paid work fail to put the needs of their children first), increased divorce rates, higher numbers of single-parent families and open homosexuality – is also blamed for increased crime rates, high unemployment and drug-taking. Society's social problems are seen as the result of the breakdown of family life. This not only stifles initiative by taking money out of the economy which could otherwise be invested productively; it penalises the 'conventional' family. For example, those who live in conventional families are penalised by higher taxation which supports those who have immoral life-styles. Indeed, it has been argued that this high tax burden makes it very difficult for a family to choose to have a wife who stays at home to care for the children. High welfare spending, necessitating high levels of taxation, forces married women into the labour market.

The New Right's Familial Ideology

The New Right's definition of the family evolved out of its reactions to the social changes of the 1960s and 1970s – out of the conservative reaction to the so-called 'permissive society'. Specifically, the pro-family movement is reacting to changes in the ways that men and women relate to each other and the roles that they play in society. The pro-family movement idealises the traditional patriarchal nuclear family – a family comprising the male bread-winner, an economically dependent female home-maker and socially and economically dependent children. Female dependency on men is seen as psychologically necessary for men:

> ... to a large extent poverty and unemployment and even the largely psychological condition of 'unemployability' are chiefly reflections of family deterioration ... Nothing is so destructive to all those male values as the growing ... recognition that when all is said and done [a man's] wife and children are better off without him. (Gilder, 1982, p. 118)

The ideal family is one in which the man sees his role as being the disciplinarian as well as the economic provider and the woman sees her role as one of sacrificing herself to the needs of household and children: 'The family is the God-ordained institution of the marriage of one man and one woman together for a lifetime with their biological or adopted children' (Falwell, 1980, p. 104).

The family is seen as God-given but also as based upon essential biological differences between men, women and children and their differing needs. Women are seen as biologically needing to be mothers and fulfilling themselves through motherhood. Biological mothering is also seen as the foundation of the social role of women, who are the ones 'naturally' committed to caring for children. Children are seen as needing family support during a prolonged childhood and parents are seen as those best able to guide their children's moral and social development.

> We believe that men and women are biologically suited to their different roles, that these are God-given and that it is within the family where fathers provide and mothers care that children are given the best, most stable and most fulfilling start to life. (Green and Webster-Gardiner, 1988, p. 9)

Thus, for the pro-family movement the patriarchal nuclear family is seen as natural and universal and other family forms are seen as deviant and immoral. Indeed, it was the realisation that 'deviant' family forms were becoming socially acceptable that led the pro-family movement to assert their definition of the family so strongly. In the 1970s in both Britain and the United States the main political parties outdid each other in their attempts to demonstrate that they were pro-family, concerned about supporting and securing family life. However, the Democrats in the United States under the leadership of Jimmy Carter and the Labour Party in Britain both accepted that a variety of family forms existed and, especially in their social and welfare policies, were concerned with establishing the ways in which the state could sustain and support *all* families. For the New Right the role of the state was to ensure the independence of the private family sphere – forcing the family to be 'free'. As such the family was to be responsible for the economic and moral welfare of its members, providing the basis for real security.

> Family policy now connotes different things for liberals and conservatives. Family policy in liberal circles is understood to mean economic assistance and social services that will put a floor under family income and lead the way to self-sufficiency. There is a tendency for conservatives to read a different meaning into national programmes directed to the family, a reading that equates family policy with acceptance of violence, promiscuity, easy abortion, casual attitudes towards marriage and divorce, natural indifference to child-rearing responsibilities. If family policy means accepting these behaviour patterns, indeed facilitating them by managing resulting economic hardship and social stigma, conservatives want none of it. For them, family policy appears to involve the use of national resources to legitimise behaviour not concomitant with behaviour typical of the American family. Right-minded national policy should reinforce traditional American patterns, but not abide deviations that smack of irresponsibility. (Steiner, 1981, p. 17)

The pro-family movements are concerned that women should fulfil a traditional role as wives and mothers. They are against women's liberation because they believe women do not have the same rights as men to work and participate in the public sphere. Women are not, in their view, equal citizens with men. 'Our nation is in serious danger when motherhood is considered a task which is undemanding, unfulfilling and boring. I believe that a woman's call to be a wife and mother is the highest calling in the world' (Falwell, 1980, pp. 106–7).

Men must be economic providers and must be controlled by having familial responsibilities. Ann Patterson, an activist against the Equal Rights Amendment, expounds views similar to those of George

Gilder (see Chapter 5) and the New Right intellectuals when she says: 'If you take away the man's responsibility to provide for the wife and children, you've taken away everything he has. A woman, after all, can do everything a man can do. And have babies. A man has awe for a woman. Men have fragile egos' (quoted in Jane O'Reilly, 'The big time players behind the small town image', *MS*, January 1983).

The New Right see the family as crucial for maintaining stability. Men are controlled by their familial responsibilities; women are controlled by husbands and children are controlled by parents. Women are to be full-time mothers socialising their children and caring for their husbands. The role of the state is to support this natural, God-given unit, not to undermine it with easy divorce, abortion, contraception for under-age girls and social security payments for single-parents. In the words of Mrs Thatcher: 'It is time to change the approach from what Government can do for people to what people can do for themselves. Time to shake off the self-doubt induced by decades of dependence on the state as master, not servant' (in a speech to the Conservative Party Conference in 1979).

Thus the New Right familial ideology is a backlash, reacting to changes in family composition and social values over the last 20 or 30 years – especially the growth of female-headed households. It argues for a form of family life that does not accord with how most people now choose to live. The popular appeal of this image of the family is that it does accord with the *ideal* of how many people think they might like to live – Mum, Dad and kids living together in harmony, Dad going out to work and Mum caring for the children. However, many people are not *able* to live in accordance with this ideal. Furthermore, the ideal itself proves not so idyllic when we examine it closely. As long ago as 1963 Betty Friedan, writing about middle-class housewives in America in the 1950s, described as 'the disease with no name' the outcome for women who endured comfortable prisons in the valium-belt suburbs at the heart of the American consumer dream. Looking at some early research into marriage, Jessie Bernard (1973) found that being a housewife can literally make women sick: they were more likely to suffer from psychological and physical illness. In Britain, Brown and Harris (1978) have documented how many women caring for young children at home suffer from depression. Rather than being 'a haven from a heartless world', the family is a place where women work hard, often suffer depression and are frequently abused physically or sexually by male relatives. Divorce and single parenthood enable women to escape from unsatisfactory relationships (though often into poverty), while having paid employment gives a measure of economic independence (though women can usually find only low-paid and low-status jobs). Public opinion polls in both Britain and the United States suggest that most people think that women should be able to have abortions if they choose. Nor is there strong opposition to homosexual and lesbian relationships.

This is not to deny that many people aspire to live in a nuclear family, nor that many feel that it is desirable for women with young children not to be in paid employment, nor that women are seen as primarily responsible for domestic labour. Indeed, earlier research by one of us indicated that among unemployed teenagers and young adults the conventional family – with marriage, a male bread-winner and an owner-occupied home – was the ideal to which they aspired even when they had no way of achieving it and when, in fact, they embarked on family life in very different ways by co-habitation and having children outside wedlock (Wallace, 1987). This is why the pro-family policies of the New Right have a popular appeal. However, the popular ideal of the family is also far from what the New Right actually want. Most people reject the idea of an authoritarian family in which the male dominates and women are treated more like children than adults. Most women now want and expect to be in paid employment outside the home for most of their married lives, even when they have dependent children (Martin and Roberts, 1984). Nor is their only motivation an economic one: women work for fulfilment, companionship and other non-economic goals.

Most important of all, perhaps, is the 'fact' that the New Right view of the family is patriarchal (that is, it serves the interests of men) and favours middle-class families; it is also racist in its implications because it has a very rigidly defined idea of what the right family form is, based upon middle-class, white ideals. Families of ethnic minorities which do not conform to this model are labelled deviant. Only middle-class families can afford to have wives or mothers who are not economically active. Working-class and black women seldom have had the luxury of choosing to opt out of paid employment.

The emphasis on nation (as opposed to society) and on Christian morality is also racist. This is because it implies that white British society and the Christian values of the Anglican Church that go with it are morally superior to those of other nations, cultures and religions. The moral superiority of Britain and the United States in relation to other nation-states is evident in such New Right writing, as is the latent racism. It is most evident in arguments on schooling (see below), but it is also implicit in the New Right's basic definition of the family. The black Afro-Caribbean matriarchal family, or the extended family of Britons of African or Asian origin or other minority groups, cannot easily be accommodated within the definition. The emphasis on the Christian basis of the family and of morality more generally is also racist – part of the cultural racism which sees white superiority in terms of culture, rather than the more traditional biological racism which focuses on supposed biological differences between people. (This is not to deny a biologicalism within New Right thinking – many New Right commentators *do* argue that the nuclear family is the biological norm.)

Because for the New Right the family is the basic building block of society, its collapse is said to have resulted in the whole moral foundation of society beginning to disintegrate. Furthermore, for the 'moral' New Right, moral and economic decline go hand in hand – a decline in morality results in economic decline. Moral decline is seen primarily as the consequence of state intervention in the 'private' sphere of the family, an intrusion that takes away the moral responsibility of individuals to provide for themselves and their families. It not only encourages dependency on the state but also encourages families to abandon responsibility for the care and economic support of disabled and elderly members. Parents abdicate responsibility for the moral and sex education of their children and cease to see it as their responsibility to control their children. Since men have less incentive to work hard to provide for their wives and children and they can easily abandon them, it leads to rising single parenthood and divorce. Women are able to live independently from men by claiming state support. Women's liberation is seen as one of the major factors lying behind these trends because it leads women to question their role in the family and undermines their willingness to sacrifice themselves to the needs of others. Consequently, married women have been less prepared to submerge themselves in domestic responsibilities and have increasingly taken paid employment for personal as well as economic reasons, thus reducing their economic dependence upon men. This means that they have insufficient time to socialise or control their children adequately. Thus while the economic New Right see the main cause of relative economic decline in Britain and the United States as state intervention in the economy, the moral New Right point to intervention in the private sphere of family life. Both are critical of government spending on welfare – the economic New Right because it results in high taxation, expensive and excessive bureaucracy and reduced incentives to work, the moral New Right because it supports immoral behaviour and discourages Victorian values of thrift, self-restraint and sobriety.

However, the moral New Right, like the economic New Right, see Britain and the United States in economic decline, losing their influence as the leading industrial nations. While the economic New Right emphasise economic factors, the moral New Right emphasise a decline in 'moral' behaviour and adherence to moral values. Both are concerned with stressing the need for governments to develop policies which will enable Britain and the United States to re-emerge as leading world nations in the 1990s – to regain their lost greatness.

Familialism and Familial Ideology: the Feminist Critique

The feminist attack on the family is a major element of New Right concern. Feminists have not only challenged the view that the patriarchal nuclear family – that is, the family of male bread-winner with a dependent wife and children – is universal and natural, but have argued that this family is the major site of the subordination of women. The first wave of feminists, in the nineteenth century, did not on the whole challenge the place of women in families, but argued for a woman's right to choose marriage and domestication *or* a career in the public world of employment. Second-wave feminists, however, have challenged the societal expectation that women who marry should become mainly carers in the domestic sphere, that they should devote themselves to the needs of their husbands and children.

Fundamental to the feminist case is the revelation that 'the family' is neither natural nor universal. Familialism is an ideology that serves to subordinate women to the needs of men and capitalism. Feminists have revealed that what was seen as natural and inevitable was socially constructed and could therefore be challenged and changed. Commonsense beliefs about the nature of the family, which were supported by dominant social-scientific theories, actually served mainly to deny women the opportunity to participate in the wider society and gain equality with men. Furthermore, both commonsense beliefs about the family and social-scientific theories concealed the extent to which different members of the family experienced family life in different ways.

Both as a political movement and as an academic area of knowledge, feminism challenged the traditional role of women and particularly women's role in the family. Feminists pointed out that the 'sovereign individual' of liberal capitalism was in fact gendered: men were constituted as sovereign individuals, but women were not – they were seen as dependants of husbands/fathers. Feminism was a challenge both to capitalism and to patriarchy; it challenged the traditional role assigned to women as carers in the domestic sphere and the view that women were naturally or religiously constituted as inferior to men. Furthermore, feminists asserted that women as individuals had rights and needs of their own that they could not be expected to subordinate to those of men and capitalism.

Feminism was seen by the New Right as a real threat to social stability in a new and more extreme form than the changes in the family which had developed in the period after World War Two, such as the increase in divorce and the increased employment of married women outside the home. Most divorcees remarried and re-formed patriarchal nuclear families; single parenthood tended to be a temporary stage between two traditional marriages. Most married women in paid employment worked hours that fitted in with their domestic responsibilities and had a period out of the labour market while their children were young. These changes did not radically question the naturalness of the family or women's role in it. Feminism did. It not only challenged the view that the family and women's role within it were natural, but argued that women should have equal rights with men in the public and the private sphere. It challenged the dominant position of men and the view that women were inferior to and therefore naturally subordinate to men. The feminist movement successfully fought for equal rights in the public sphere – in employment, in education and so on – and argued for a restructuring of the domestic sphere so that men and women shared responsibility for domestic work and childcare.

The New Right fears that such changes will endanger the stability of society – reacting to the changes they perceive as already having taken place. They argue that feminism has played a major role in what they see as the breakdown of the traditional family and the idea that there is only one acceptable family form. The welfare state has also played a key role in these processes, according to the New Right. It enables women with dependent children to live independent of a man, by providing basic income support. This means that men no longer have a responsibility to provide for their families and removes a major incentive for them to seek and retain paid employment. Children brought up without a father's discipline and role model, the New Right argue, are likely to become the next generation of welfare dependants. Further, the high levels of taxation needed to finance the welfare state mean that many women with children are forced to take paid employment in order to maintain an adequate standard of living for their families.

It is important to stress that the New Right are arguing for a return to what they see as the traditional family form: an independent, mutually self-supporting family with the husband/father as the bread-winner and the wife/mother as the home-maker, both providing for dependent children; a family where parents take responsibility for the moral, social and economic support of their children and the father is clearly respected as the head. They perceive this 'natural' family as having been undermined by feminism and the welfare state. The family is seen to be the foundation of a strong, moral society and to be essential for the maintenance of capitalism. This view of family and family life is central to New Right thought.

The Moral and the Economic New Right: Origins and Articulation

Within New Right thinking in Britain and the United States at least two not wholly consistent strands of thought have been discerned. On the one hand, economic liberalism advocates a minimum role for the state and a free market economy. Economic liberalism argues that the government cannot and should not intervene in the economy, nor in the lives of individuals unless they endanger the rights of others. There is a strong emphasis on the fundamental freedom and rights of all individuals. These *laissez-faire* ideas have had greater influence under Thatcherism and Reaganomics than was the case in the post-World War Two era of welfare expansion.

On the other hand, other traditional authoritarian conservatives tend to believe that good behaviour can only be ensured through the maintenance of a strong centralised state with a commitment to law and order and nationhood. Furthermore, these traditional 'authoritarian' Tories tend to favour the continuation of traditional patterns of authority and to stress obedience and subservience to traditional principles. They stress Christian values and the conventional family as providing the solid foundation for society. They oppose ideas and movements which might threaten such institutions.

The representation of the family is important in understanding how this contradiction can be maintained, because it is through the family that people look after other members of the community; it is the family which puts moral restraints on rampant self-interest. However, the family has to be constructed in such a way that children and women are seen as the dependants of men (rather than the state) in order for this to work. Furthermore, the family and the traditional gender division of labour is one way in which traditional, Victorian values are maintained. In many ways the moral New Right with its strong conservative roots apparently contradicts the arguments of classical liberalism. However, in practice the two ideologies have accommodated each other. As Desmond King (1987) puts it:

> ... each strand gains something from joining with the other. Liberalism is the source of the New Right's economic and political theories and policy objectives; conservatism provides a set of residual claims to cover the consequences of pursuing liberal policies. For example, the liberal objectives of reducing public welfare provision implies a traditional role for women and the family; conservatives provide an ideology justifying such outcomes from public policy. Conservatives provide liberals with a coherent theory of the state, absent from their own theories. Both ideologies fear the extension of social citizenship

rights and therefore are united in their criticisms of the welfare state. (p. 25)

King suggests that the articulation of the liberal theory of a free-market economy and a liberal state with the conservative emphasis on authority and public order leads in practice to a strong government which emphasises law and order and familial values, but a limited state that plays little direct role in the market. More importantly, he points out that

It is not coincidental that economic doctrines advocating a minimal state involvement in the economy should be promoted in unison with an attack on the negative and undesirable effects of the welfare state. To implement New Right liberal doctrines required retrenching the welfare state, conservative arguments about the latter's harmful moral and social effects complemented such economic policies. (p. 50)

This is not to suggest, however, that New Right ideology is entirely coherent, nor that there is necessarily a unity between New Right thinkers. While liberalism has obviously influenced contemporary political practices of the New Right, especially in the area of economic policies – monetarism in Britain and 'Reaganomics' in the United States – the major influence is conservatism. The New Right are strongly committed to *laissez-faire* economic policies, but also to the conservative emphasis on tradition and hierarchy rather than the liberal emphasis on autonomy and the fundamental equality of autonomous individuals. The emphasis on the family is also clearly tied to conservatism, with the family seen as the basic building block of an organic social order. While the liberal emphasis on the individual would seem to be gender-neutral and not to stress primary organisations such as the family, the liberal tradition is not wholly consistent about this. On the whole, both historical and contemporary liberal thinkers pay little attention to the family and tend not to consider women explicitly. However, with some notable exceptions, liberal theory is at best sex-blind and at worst sexist, explicitly constructing *men* (as opposed to all adults) as autonomous individuals. Enlightenment thinkers rejected in theory the notion of the patriarch as ruler and the family as ordained by God. While there is no reason why men and women, husbands and wives should *not* be seen as equal in liberal thought, in practice Enlightenment thinkers tended to argue that natural differences between men and women meant that men would generally be in charge. They also assumed that women naturally were the carers in the domestic sphere. The moral New Right tend to stress the God-given nature of the family, but biological bases for it also underpin some New Right thinking in this area.

The two key influences on New Right thinking, then, are conservatism, with its emphasis on tradition and hierarchy, and liberal economic theory – that is, *laissez-faire*. There is less emphasis in New Right thought than in traditional liberal political theory on individual freedom with respect to morals or on natural rights. The New Right is best conceptualised as a backlash movement, reacting to social changes that have taken place since World War Two, especially in the areas of morality, welfare spending and the role of women. Although it seems radical, in fact it is a reassertion of political and economic ideologies that were dominant in Britain and the United States throughout the nineteenth and early twentieth centuries. Modern New Right conservatism in both countries combines a nostalgia for the past with a zeal to save the nations from what is perceived as their current economic and moral sickness, a sickness predominantly caused by economic policies in the period after World War Two, and by welfarism and rights movements – particularly feminism. While the major economists who have influenced the policies of the New Right are inheritors of classical liberal traditions and explicitly reject conservatism (see, for example, Green, 1987), modern conservatism nevertheless can be seen to be the inheritor of nineteenth-century conservative thought.

Conservatism as a political ideology developed as a reaction to Enlightenment thought in the late eighteenth century in the writings of, for example, John Adams in the United States, Edmund Burke in The United Kingdom and Joseph LeMaitre in France. These writers challenged the Enlightenment belief in human perfectibility and rejected the argument that reason could replace that which had been tested by experience. These conservative writers rejected the liberal view that the individual preceded society and argued that individuals could not be understood except in the context of the society in which they lived. Society was seen as being made up not of fundamentally equal and free individuals but of social institutions and groups of which the most basic was the family. Within the family, as in society, there was a hierarchy of authority – at the family apex was the father, and at the state apex was the monarch. Claims to authority and loyalty rested in inherited custom, not rational principles. Individual freedom (liberty) was guaranteed by custom, tradition and the past, not by 'natural rights'.

While the conservative thinkers of the late eighteenth century rejected liberal political theory, they did not reject the idea of the minimal state, especially in terms of economic policies. Edmund Burke accepted the new science of *laissez-faire* economics. Burke argued that the state should not intervene in the economy or protect the poor against the harsh realities of economic competition. Libertarian conservatism – the articulation of conservative political thought with *laissez-faire* economic principles – dominated the British Conservative (Tory) Party throughout the nineteenth and early twentieth centuries. In the period after World War Two the domination of the Party in Britain passed to 'organic' conservatives who, while stressing tradition and hierarchy, also argued that the wealthy and powerful had a responsibility for the welfare of the less fortunate members of society. These conservatives all but abandoned *laissez-faire* and endorsed proposals for social reform and welfarism – becoming what some commentators have called 'reluctant collectivists'.

The rise of the New Right as a dominant political force in Britain and the United States represents the return to dominance in the British Conservative Party and the United States Republican Party of libertarian conservatism. These conservatives are committed to tradition and authority as well as *laissez-faire* economic policies. While they share with political liberals a basic belief in a free-market economy, they reject the liberal view that society is comprised of morally and economically independent individuals imbued with a belief in the values of self-discipline. They argue for a strong state to maintain traditional moral and familial values and believe that in a free-market economy many people fail to acquire either wealth or the bourgeois virtues of self-discipline and self-help. Some individuals, as a consequence of their laziness, inability or ignorance, will fail to grasp the opportunities that are open to them. Consequently, poverty is seen as moral as well as economic failure. Morally deficient individuals are seen not only as a threat to political stability but as a potentially corrupting influence upon their families and neighbourhoods, necessitating policies designed to reinforce traditional moral values. This explains the emphasis in Britain under Thatcher and in the US under Reagan on the free market but the strong state.

One should not assume from this simple picture, however, that the New Right is a unified political movement with a coherent political ideology. Thinkers and activists who have gathered under the broad umbrella of the New Right represent a diverse set of ideas that often conflict with each other. Individual groups and organisations that have been referred to as New Right cover a broad spectrum of ideas from libertarian conservatism to classical liberalism and include those who stress economic policies as well as others whose major emphasis is on traditional moral values. While Thatcherism and Reaganism are influenced by elements of classical liberal thought, traditional conservatism and *laissez-faire* economics, they can also be seen as the inheritors of a strong conservative tradition, libertarian conservatism.

To conclude: the dominant influence in New Right thinking, in terms of images of the family, is the conservative one. Indeed, the moral New Right has to a large extent been not only predominantly conservative but also influenced by Christian ideas. However, as we have indicated above, elements of the New Right justify traditional familialism on biological rather than religious grounds. The New Right, then, are dramatically opposed to changes in the role and status of women – especially married women – that have been occurring over the last three decades. However, while they want a strong state to reinforce traditional values, they also argue that state policies (especially in the area of welfare) are what has helped to undermine the traditional family. Consequently they agree with the economic New Right that the state should be rolled back in the area of welfare. Policies based on New Right ideas are likely, therefore, to have an influence on families and family life. This comes about not just because of the image of the family in New Right thought, but also because of the impact of changes in economic policy on families. Indeed, as we shall argue in the next chapter, the New Right image of the family differs little from what has been dominant in British politics and underpinned the welfare state and the relative consensus over economic and welfare policies that was dominant in Britain and the United States in the period after World War Two.

2
Welfarism and Welfare States: Securing the Patriarchal Family

In Chapter 1 we have argued that the New Right has a specific image of the family – the patriarchal nuclear family – which, it argues, is both natural and inevitable. The New Right also argues that a strong state is necessary to ensure the stability of this family form. Welfare and moral policies of successive governments in Britain and the United States are seen as having undermined and endangered it, while feminists and other radicals have challenged its naturalness. Not only do these policies enable and these discourses encourage the growth of 'unnatural' families and life-styles, but welfare policy more generally has undermined the role of the family as the provider of welfare. Welfare has become a public rather than a private matter, eroding the power that private welfare allows families to exert over family members and in particular inducing men to abandon their role as economic supporters of their families. However, the New Right justify their attack on the welfare state not only in terms of familial discourse but also because of their *laissez-faire* economic policies. They argue that state-provided welfare is inefficient, ineffective and liable to discourage individual effort by reducing the incentives for hard work.

Because this way of regarding welfare has to some extent 'captured the agenda', critiques of New Right policies on welfare have frequently appeared to be defending the welfare state as defined in its entirety by the so-called 'welfare consensus'. Welfare collectivism is defended against the individualism of the New Right (see, for example, Gamble, 1988). Particularly important in this defence has been the re-assertion of the rights of social citizenship – rights to the collective provision of welfare for all members of society. Attacks on welfare provision are attacks not only on basic income maintenance but also on what has been called the 'social wage' – the myriad services provided by the state to meet the needs of all citizens or of specific groups. Opponents of New Right welfare policies often have found themselves in the paradoxical position of defending a social welfarism of which they themselves have been critical. Frequently, this defence seems to gloss over the classism, partriarchalism, racism and ageism inherent in the 'welfare consensus' and the way that the welfare state was constituted in practice as a means of social control (see Squires, 1990).

In defending state welfare we cannot ignore the fact that it exerts a form of control as well as providing social citizenship rights, nor that the welfare state is as much about protecting the interests of the powerful as it is about meeting the needs of the disadvantaged. As Squires (1990) points out,

> ... in welfare capitalist societies ... welfare develops an almost schizophrenic duality. On the one hand it approximates to an idea of the 'general' welfare of society – usually subordinated to the particular interests, the wealth and well-being of the more affluent sections of society. On the other hand it comes to refer to the specific measures, institutions and policies designed to handle the casualties of this society. There are, therefore, two welfares, the one that stands as a symbol of the well being of the wealthy, of social order and harmony, and the welfare of the poor which pursues these same goals by coercion when it fails to attain them by compliance. (p. 40)

Steadman Jones (1971) makes the point even more forcefully:

> Looking forward to the creation of the Welfare State [historians] have concentrated upon proposals for old age pensions, free education, free school meals, subsidised housing and 'national insurance'. They have virtually ignored parallel proposals to segregate the casual poor, to establish detention centres for 'loafers', to separate pauper children from 'degenerate' parents or to ship the 'residuum' overseas. Yet, for contemporaries, both sorts of proposal composed parts of a single debate.

To criticise how welfare was constituted in practice, however, is entirely compatible with defending its provision in theory, and many of those who are most critical of how collective welfare has been structured and delivered are even more opposed to the New Right attack on its provision even in principle.

Despite our references to the so-called 'welfare consensus' of Britain and the United States in the period after World War Two, we should note that the nature of welfare and the role of the state in providing it has always been contested (see, for example, Clarke *et al.* 1987). Also, the 'consensus' was between political elites and does not mean that there was a normative consensus in the general population about the means or ends of welfare and welfare policies. While the affluence of the period after World War Two might have suggested 'an end of ideology', in fact the architects of the welfare state in Britain were reluctant collectivists (see Chapter 1), while the Great Society programmes in the United States were never meant to provide collectivist welfare. Welfare policies in both countries were not intended to legislate for a more equal society, but to provide a safety net, acknowledging that a functioning market economy produces social casualties. They were designed to maintain existing social relationships, assuming that hierarchy and inequalities were both necessary and inevitable. This is not to deny that disadvantaged groups did benefit from them, nor that cutting welfare programmes is an attack on the well being of these groups. It is to suggest, however, that welfare and welfarism form an area of contestation and that the beginning of the period of 'welfare consensus' rested on a fragile coalition – a coalition that was endangered once the economic growth and expansion of the 1950s and 1960s came to a halt in Britain and the United States.

The welfare state did not challenge traditional ideologies of the family. Indeed, as Elizabeth Wilson (1977) has pointed out, state interventions in the family have been designed precisely to construct and sustain the patriarchal nuclear family form. Welfare policies have assumed that the patriarchal family of employed husband with dependent wife and children is how people do and should arrange their lives. The male-dominated political Left has been as concerned as the political Right to reinforce the position of the man in the family and the dependency of wives. This is the case not only in terms of income maintenance policies, where married women were not granted economic citizenship – that is, the same entitlement as men and single women (see, for example, Summers, 1991) – but in the fight for the 'family wage' and in the 'creation' of the mother's role – state intervention in the family being legitimated in terms of ensuring that mothers carried out their childcare roles adequately (see, for example, Williams, 1989; Abbott and Wallace, 1990a,b). Those who legislated for social welfarism, however, saw the state as helping families to perform their social functions more adequately. Social welfarism was seen as securing and sustaining the patriarchal nuclear family.

What the New Right argue is that state welfare has had unintended and undesirable consequences, and that it has undermined the family form that its proponents wanted to support and sustain. The welfare state has enabled parents, and particularly fathers, to abandon their responsibility for the financial support and moral education of their children and wives. It has engendered an easy faith that 'the state will provide' and undermined notions of self-help and self-sufficiency. Furthermore, in some areas – for example, in the education system – it has replaced the family and specifically fathers as controllers of children. This has resulted in a decline in moral standards, an increase in delinquency and crime, a rejection of the Protestant work ethic and the creation of an underclass of welfare dependants.

In the 1960s and 1970s debates took place around welfare and welfare policies that resulted in certain changes that have been especially attacked by the New Right. These debates and reforms were primarily concerned with the patriarchalism of state policies in Britain and the United States. The apparent outcome of these conflicts was significant advances for women. However, in practice these advances have been more symbolic than real (see Abbott and Wallace, 1990a), and some changes, such as the increased employment of married women, probably owe more to the restructuring of capitalism and the creation of part-time 'jobs for women' than to changes in women's status. Employment for women often means only that public patriarchy replaces private patriarchy (Walby, 1990).

This is true not only in the area of paid employment but also in women's encounters with the welfare state, where the state replaces the husband in policing behaviour. A notable example has been the British DSS policing of co-habitation. In Britain, for income support purposes a man and woman living together as if married have their resources aggregated in precisely the same way as a married couple. An unmarried woman who lives with a man (or in some cases has a sexual relationship with a man who stays overnight in her accomodation regulary) is not entitled to claim benefits because she is considered to be his financial dependant. Discourses of motherhood and women's caring role also inform the ways in which a plethora of state representatives, including teachers, health visitors, district nurses and social workers, judge women. They work with a set of expectations of how women should behave as wives, mothers and informal carers. When a mother is thought to have 'failed', the state steps in. (The New Right want the father to be held responsible.)

We should recognise, therefore, that the welfare state was explicitly designed to support and sustain the patriarchal nuclear family – a family form that is the site of the subordination and exploitation of women. It is not difficult to find relevant criticisms of the ways in which welfare has been structured and delivered in Britain and the United States. However, it is vital also to recognise that welfare policies have nonetheless been instrumental in helping the most dis- advantaged members of society – including women and children. The state provision of education ensures that all children have the oppor- tunity of reaching a minimum educational standard, the state provision of income support acts as a safety net, and health services (especially in Britain) have helped improve the health of women and children. Thus we would argue that cutbacks in state welfare provision actually undermine the ability of families to care and provide for their members. In order to understand the ways in which New Right ideas and policies have impacted on families, it is necessary to understand the ways in which social policies in Britain and the United States have helped families since World War Two. This is what we proceed to outline in the rest of the chapter.

Social Change and Social Policy in Britain

The moral and economic climate of Britain after World War Two did represent a departure from the pre-war situation. In the post-war period a range of legislation was introduced which laid the foundations for a comprehensive welfare state. At the same time there was a parliamentary consensus that the government should intervene in the economy to maintain full employment of men and single women. The Beveridge Report of 1942 set the basic framework for the welfare state based upon a Keynesian economic model for managing the economy. The report asserted that the government should be responsible for maintaining full employment and that economic growth could be managed and stabilised by government intervention in the economy. These ideas were broadly supported by both Conservative and Labour Parties, who agreed that the state should guarantee a minimal level of welfare for its citizens as a matter of right and should use demand management to stabilise the economy. These ideas underpinned economic and social policy until the mid-1970s and critics, especially on the right, had little influence. The debates that took place, were over the detailed matters of policy rather than over the desirability of the welfare state itself – for example, debates about the *amount* of public housing being built rather than about whether or not it should be built at all, about the organisation of the National Health Service rather than about replacing it with a private health care system, and about whether married women should have full economic citizenship. This period has generally been referred to as 'the era of welfare consensus'.

The welfare state was built in the 1940s round certain assumptions about the family and specifically women's roles in it: that women would get married and that once married they would be economically dependent upon their husbands for the rest of their lives. The primary duty of married women was to care for their children and husbands. The policy of full employment would ensure that husbands and fathers could provide for wives and children. As Beveridge put it:

All women by marriage acquire a new economic and social status with rights and risks different from those of the unmarried. On marriage a woman gains a legal right to maintenance by the husband as a first line of defence against the risks which fall directly on the solitary woman. She undertakes at the same time to perform vital unpaid service and becomes exposed to new risks, including the risk that her married life may be ended prematurely by widowhood or separation. (Beveridge, 1942, p. 49)

Women who lost their economic provider – by, for example, being widowed or divorced or abandoned – would have recourse to state benefits. Widows' benefits were classed as a contributory benefit, having been paid for by the husband's honestly earned National Insurance contributions. On the other hand, women who were seen as mainly responsible for their situation (such as divorcees) would have to live on income maintenance – provided by the stigmatising means-tests of the National Assistance Board – which was paid only at the lowest subsistence rate. Consequently, there were higher benefit rates for deserving widows than for undeserving divorcees, and Beveridge considered this legitimate in order to discourage irresponsible behaviour. Women who had children without being married were seen as so aberrant at the time that they did not merit a mention as part of the normal family pattern, presumably because most gave up their children for adoption or concealed them in some way within a 'normal' family.

In the period after 1948, welfare spending grew steadily until it constituted 30.3 per cent of Gross Domestic Product (GDP) by 1960 and 44.6 per cent of GDP by 1980. This represented a considerable commitment to public expenditure financed primarily from the progressive taxation of employees and taxation of profit and wealth. This expenditure helped to pay for a programme of public house-building, an expanded health service and an expanded education system, which not only provided universal education up to the age of 16 but also extended training and higher education for an increasing proportion of the age-group. Children's departments were set up by local authorities and later, following the 1968 Seebohm Report, were replaced by expanded social service departments. These departments implemented the 1969 Children and Young Persons Act which legislated for the non-custodial care of children and gave social workers an enhanced role in monitoring young offenders and in intervention in the family. The atmosphere of welfare reform which pervaded the 1960s was reflected also in a range of education reports concerned with improving the opportunities of the disadvantaged youngster (although always with the argument that this would help to improve economic performance). This helped to strengthen a trend towards liberal, child-centered theories of learning which were influential in the teacher training college, focusing on state education as a benign form of compensation for the disadvantages of family backgrounds.

However, the central element of the welfare state established in Britain in 1948 was that of income maintenance. There were two components to this – contributory and non-contributory benefits. The former were paid as of right to those who met the relevant contributory conditions, while the latter were means-tested. Thus employees, employers and the state paid contributions to insure workers against unemployment, sickness, industrial injury, disability and old age. The non-contributory, mainly means-tested benefits originally called National Assistance and now referred to as Social Security, were intended originally as an interim measure until the majority became eligible for contributory benefits. (In both types of benefit, the amount of benefit payable and the criteria of eligibility are laid down by central government.) However, in reality, the number of people wholly or partly dependent on non-contributory benefits has increased since the 1940s and the range of these benefits has likewise increased. Far from being an 'interim measure', non-contributory social security now provides for the largest proportion of welfare expenditure, and it is this trend which contributes to the argument that welfare spending has somehow got out of control. These claimants, because they have not 'contributed' to their benefits through national insurance or have exhausted their entitlement to contributory benefits, are seen as the less deserving.

A number of benefits targeted specifically at families (that is, those with children) were introduced in 1948 and more have been added subsequently. The most important at present are: the universal child benefit paid to a mother for each of her children; one-parent benefit paid to lone parents in addition to child benefit; and family income supplement (now income support) paid to low income families where the parent(s) are in paid employment but earn less than a defined minimum needs level for their size of family.

The welfare state in Britain provides nearly free health care and education to all of its citizens. A variety of different benefits – contributory and means-tested – ensure that all citizens (with the exception of married women, who are treated for the most part as dependents of their husbands) are eligible for state income maintenance if they are unable to work because of age, illness, disability or the unavailability of paid employment. In addition they may be eligible for benefits towards housing costs and pay a reduced rate of community charge (local tax).

There is no official 'poverty line' in Britain, but benefit levels have frequently been taken to indicate a poverty line. Many commentators argue that people are relatively poor if they have an income less than 40 per cent above means-tested benefit levels (Townsend, 1979). This view of the social security safety net fostered the emergence of the idea that poverty was 'relative' rather than 'absolute' and that the state was ultimately responsible for the well-being of all of its citizens. This, along with the rising levels of post-war affluence, encouraged expectations of ever-improving living standards. Women went to work to staff the expanding service industries and to help pay for better living standards; by 1987 46 per cent of all women with children were in paid employment outside the home, as were 30 per cent of women with children younger than two years. This working pattern was also facilitated by the smaller family size made possible with the development of the contraceptive pill and the compression of the child-bearing years into a relatively short span of the life-course. Motherhood is therefore no longer a full-time job for many women. In the public sphere there was recognition of women's economic contribution through the Equal Pay Act of 1970 (implemented in 1975) and the Equal Opportunities Act of 1975. (For more details of this legislation see Gregory, 1987.)

These changes created a climate within which ideas about sexuality and gender roles were questioned more generally. A series of acts passed during the 1950s and 1960s were thought to herald a new era of 'permissiveness' which was seen as a form of liberation. The change in the censorship laws following the celebrated obscenity trial of *Lady Chatterley's Lover* in 1959 was fought for by distinguished artists in the name of artistic freedom and the abolition of so-called 'Victorian prudery'. The 1968 Theatres Act gave similar freedom to the stage. Consequently, during the 1960s and 1970s there were a series of stage performances featuring public shows of nudity, sex and drug-taking – for example, in shows such as 'Hair' and 'Oh Calcutta'. It was possible to buy sex manuals which advocated a loosening of inhibitions and encouragement of experimental sex. This all made the 1960s appear 'permissive', even though most people were not affected by it. There is no evidence that most people's behaviour was any more promiscuous than in previous generations. However, an atmosphere developed in which the limits of what was considered acceptable for publication and distribution became more and more widely interpreted despite the persistence of some censorship laws. Consequently, more and more explicit soft porn magazines could be bought over the counter in newsagents and advertising increasingly used provocative and incipiently pornographic portrayals of female sexuality to sell products. The growth in the number of home videos has provided ways of circumventing the censorship laws in the cinema, and depictions of sex, horror and violence have proved to be very popular forms of home entertainment. Jeffreys (1990) suggests that what began as a noble artistic struggle for freedom of expression opened the doors to the commercial exploitation of female sexuality in new and multifarious forms. Changes in the censorship laws were accompanied by the 1967 Sexual Offences Act, which recognised some limited rights for male homosexuals although it by no means sanctioned homosexual activities more generally. The campaigns by gay rights activists which began in the 1970s have attempted to obtain for gay and lesbian sexuality the same recognition as heterosexuality and have also served to make these forms of sexuality more visible.

Other legislation on abortion and divorce affected women's roles within the family more directly. The 1969 Divorce Act contributed to the divorce rate doubling between 1970 and 1980. It continued to increase at 12.5 per cent per year in the 1980s and by the mid-1980s divorce ended 37 per cent of marriages. According to Kiernan and Wicks (1990), one in five children will experience a parental divorce before the age of 16. 'Illegitimate' births have risen to 25 per cent of all live births in 1990 from just 8 per cent in 1971 and 12 per cent as recently as 1980 (although much of this is accounted for by an increased number of co-habiting couples having children – children being born in a quasi-marital situation). There has also been a three-fold increase in co-habitation between 1979 and 1987.

There is a growing number of single-parent families resulting both from more divorce and from the fact that single women who have children are more easily able to keep them. Whatever the reasons, 16 per cent of families with dependent children are headed by a lone parent (in 90 per cent of these cases a female), whereas the figure for 1961 was just 6 per cent. At the same time the number of abortions rose following the 1967 Abortion Act which made abortion more freely available (although still subject to medical control rather than women's choice), so that in 1989 14 per cent of all conceptions ended in legal medical abortion as opposed to just 6.7 per cent in 1971.

Finally, the increase in divorce and 'illegitimacy' has led to increasing numbers of women in poverty, many of whom are dependent on the welfare state. This increases the cost of welfare provision and is seen by the New Right as placing a burden on tax payers.

The moral New Right, reacting to these changes, started to become more vocal and gain more publicity in the early 1970s. For example, the *Black Papers* (published between 1970 and 1977) argued against liberal educational methods, and Mary Whitehouse and others campaigned for more censorship of sex and violence in the media (Tracey and Morrison, 1979). The debate about the treatment of young offenders came to centre on how to punish them for their crimes rather than on how to reform them, following action by more right-wing groups such as the Magistrates Association. There was a general questioning of the principles of welfare expansion and liberalisations, in which the New Right formed one – fairly isolated – voice.

This voice was heard more clearly during the economic crisis of the 1970s, when world recession and the rise in oil prices caused a major slump in the British economy. In 1979 the election to office of the Conservative Party, led by Mrs Thatcher, represented a culmination of New Right campaigning and a new era of economic and social policy.

Political and Social Change in the US

In the US the New Right were also reacting against growing welfare spending and what was perceived as the new moral climate. As in Britain, the US in the 1960s had witnessed what is often portrayed as a sexual revolution, with women's rights and gay rights movements, pre-marital sex and extra-marital sex being more publicly displayed and discussed, as well as increasing divorce and crime rates. Those who saw this as evidence of the moral decline of society blamed the family and the welfare state. In America as in Britain, there have been changes in the family. The divorce rate is comparable to Britain's, but the prevalence of single-parent families – mainly female headed – is much higher at about 20 per cent. A high percentage of women are in the labour force, as is the case in Britain, but those with young and pre-school-aged children are more likely to be in paid employment than in Britain. In 1985 just over 50 per cent of women with children under 6 years and about 65 per cent of those with children aged 6–17 years were in paid employment in the US (Ellwood, 1988, Fig. 3.2, p. 49). The comparable figures for Britain in 1988 were 36 per cent of women with a child under 5 years and 65 per cent of those with a youngest child over 5 years (Currie, 1990, p. 12).

In the US as many as one in four children live with only one parent (9 out of 10 of these being women) because of divorce, separation or the fact that the mother has never married. Thus in 1970 43 per cent of women who were the sole heads of families were widows, whereas by 1985 widowhood was the reason in only 27 per cent of such cases while in 38 per cent divorce was to blame (US Bureau of Statistics 1987, p.49). Although only 6 per cent of children live in families headed by never-married women, numbers have increased more than six-fold since 1970 and more than doubled between 1980 and 1985 (US Bureau of Census, 1986, p. 72; see Currie and Skolnick, 1988).

The United States has never developed a 'welfare state' of the type found in Britain. While it has a free and universal system of primary and secondary education, there is no National Health Service, and income maintenance for those not covered by contributory benefits is limited in coverage to certain defined needy groups. Mishra (1981) has referred to this as a 'residual welfare system'. Furthermore, the United States is a federation, which means that the states have considerable autonomy both in the ways in which they administer federal legislation and in pursuing their own legislation.

As in Britain, the major focus of attack by the New Right has been on income maintenance policies – particularly non-contributory ones. There are two main types of benefit – contributory and non-contributory. The former are generally referred to as 'Social Security' and provide insured benefits for the elderly, the totally disabled, families of deceased workers with children and the unemployed (there are no state schemes for sickness or maternity benefit). As in Britain, entitlement to these benefits is based on past employment and earnings records. Unemployment benefit is for a limited period (26 weeks as opposed to 52 weeks in Britain) and is dependent on demonstrating a genuine commitment to finding employment and proving that the last employment was not left voluntarily or as a result of being sacked. However, as in Britain, welfare spending has increased rapidly since World War Two and is seen by the New Right as a burden on tax payers, encouraging and supporting immoral life-styles and undermining the traditional family. A sharp distinction is made between what are seen as the deserving and the undeserving poor – a legacy from nineteenth-century poor laws. In both countries, most criticism is levelled at the non-contributory means-tested benefits.

Social policy in the United States originates from the measures passed by Franklin D. Roosevelt as part of the 'New Deal' in response to the economic depression of the 1930s. The Social Security Act in 1935 laid down the basic legislative framework; in 1939 it was extended to cover a wider range of workers and a greater emphasis was placed on the 'social' adequacy of insurance benefit payments. This legislation introduced three kinds of welfare insurance: unemployment compensation, old age assistance and aid to dependent children. It was framed according to the language and ideology of private insurance, and according to Achenbaum (1986) this precluded the possibility of establishing any kind of collectivist or community responsibility for misfortune. At the same time it introduced the distinction between the deserving claimants of welfare who had paid contributions and those who had not paid contributions and were living on state 'hand-outs'. In the US as in Britain, the majority of those who have not had regular employment careers are women (who have to claim through their husbands – if any) and marginalised workers who are excluded from contributory benefits schemes. The legislation was also underpined by an explicit familial ideology:

> Safeguarding the family against economic hazards is one of the major purposes of modern social legislation. Old-age legislation, contributory and non-contributory unemployment compensation, mothers' aid and general relief by several states and their political subdivisions, aid to the blind and incapacitated, all have an important bearing on preserving the family life. (*Congressional Record*, 10 June 1930, p. 6764, quoted in Achenbaum, 1986, p. 33)

From 1940 to 1972 the US welfare system grew incrementally. For example, the response to World War Two was to introduce the Serviceman's Readjustment Act which provided a mortgage and jobs for returning servicemen – a strategy targeted exclusively at men. In 1950 a 77 per cent rise was granted by President Truman. Also in the 1950s more people were made eligible for old age insurance pensions (called OASI) and also for Assistance Pensions (non-contributory OAAS), but pensions were to reflect differential earnings and were given to particular groups of workers only.

The main means-tested benefits – referred to as 'welfare'- were originally available mainly to the aged and the disabled (not entitled to contributory insurance-based Social Security benefits) and to single-parent families (or two-parent families in which the father was disabled). These benefits were federally imposed (but state-administered), based upon strict means-testing and providing very low levels of assistance. It was assumed, as in Britain, that these programmes were transitional and that the majority eventually would be covered by insurance-based Social Security – the elderly and disabled receiving benefits on the basis of their past employment records and widows' benefits being based upon the past employment of their husbands. (It was assumed that most single-parent families would be formed as a result of bereavement.) The 1935 legislation also introduced Aid for Dependent Children (ADC) to replace the mothers' and widows' pension programmes that had been introduced by most states in the early twentieth century. It was assumed after the introduction of the 1939 legislation that ADC was a temporary measure, and that eventually all fatherless children would be entitled to survivors' pensions. ADC replaced state widows' and mothers' pensions but perpetuated the stigma, means-testing and parsimony associated with them. ADC paid only for the child's upkeep, but in 1950 an amendment provided payment to the child's caretaker. The 'suitable parent' rules associated with the mothers'/widows' pension programmes continued – that is, that women continually had to demonstrate that they were fit parents by not going out, managing their budgets and not drinking, or else their children could be removed from them by welfare workers. As the number of single (non-married) mothers increased in the post-World War Two period a 'man in the house' or 'substitute parent' rule was introduced: any man with whom a recipient of ADC had a steady relationship was expected to support her and her children.

Changes in welfare policy came with the 'War on Poverty' or 'Great Society' programmes of the 1960s, introduced by President Johnson following civil rights agitation. The influence of Keynesian economics had been weaker in the US, as had the influence of left-wing ideas and policies, but the 'War on Poverty' introduced a programme of welfare reforms with influential sympathisers put in charge of programmes. This resulted in an expansion in welfare and Social Security spending, which rose from 6.9 per cent of national income in 1960 to 15 per cent in 1976. However, the percentage of national income spent on means-tested benefit for the non-elderly and non-disabled already receiving very low benefits rose from only 0.5 per cent in 1960 to 1.6 per cent in 1976, declining to 1.3 per cent by 1984 (Ellwood, 1988, Table 2.1, p. 32). In the 1960s the initial focus was on removing the barriers that prevented people from gaining employment, and programmes were introduced such as the Job Corps that trained out-of-school youth, Head Start to provide pre-school education for disadvantaged children, and 'affirmative action' and anti-discrimination programmes. The reforms included the Manpower Development and Training Act introduced in 1962 and amended in 1963 and 1968, implementing programmes aimed at improving the employment chances of disadvantaged minorities. A public welfare amendment in 1962 also provided the funding for day care facilities for the children of employed welfare mothers (that is, those receiving Aid to Families with Dependent Children), and when the Work Incentives Program was introduced in 1969 child day care was included as a support service. In 1965 the Older Americans Act extended the provision for financial and health hazards for the elderly. However, the flagship of the new legislation was Medicare, introduced in 1965 as a low-cost insurance scheme to provide medical care for the elderly, and Medicaid for those who qualified for public assistance (that is, means-tested benefits). Social Security benefits rose and unemployment insurance was extended to cover far more workers. In 1974 under the SSI (Supplementary Security Income programme) the federal government took over most of the responsibility for administering and increasing welfare benefit for older people and disabled people, but eligibility was not expanded.

In 1962 ADC became AFDC (Aid for Families with Dependent Children). The eligibility criteria for AFDC were expanded in 1969 (and again in 1972), the benefit levels increased, the man-in-the-house rule was abolished and earnings were no longer deducted dollar for dollar. At the same time, fairly generous 'earnings disregards' for childcare and work expenses were introduced. In some cases in some states, two-parent families with an unemployed adult could qualify for assistance, although eligibility criteria were still tightly drawn. However, it remained a benefit primarily for single mothers and states were given complete discretion over benefit levels.

A major change in welfare provision during the 1960s was the introduction of food stamps – available to all poor persons (those with incomes below the official poverty line) – but the benefit was low and was cut as income rose. A family with no other income received about

75 cents per person per meal in 1986. As David Ellwood (1988) points out, after the 'War on Poverty' programme was completed

> ... there was a guaranteed income, but it was in the form of Food Stamps that were worth at most $3,300 per year (in 1986 dollars). To get any kind of serious income support, families usually still had to be aged, disabled or headed by a single parent. (p.138)

Various 'community action' programmes were also introduced as part of the 'Great Society' reforms aimed at deprived communities. However, after 1966 the reforms began to falter. New initiatives were rejected if they required more funds or any new bureaucratic structure and the American welfare system, which had grown incrementally, came to be regarded as 'a mess'. Middle-class voters were frustrated by the piecemeal and confusing reforms and there were fears of people being able to take advantage of the system; the US social security system, like the British one, was haunted by the spectre of the 'welfare scrounger'. Plans under Presidents Nixon and Carter to replace the existing welfare system with a more comprehensive social security programme, including a minimum wage, were scrapped; instead the eligibility criteria were tightened up and benefits more strongly linked to work incentives and targeted at 'deserving' cases.

In 1972, however, there was a 20 per cent increase in pension benefits, and Medicare was extended to the under 65s if they were disabled. After 1975 benefits paid under the Supplementary Security Income programme were cumulatively adjusted in line with yearly increases in the cost of living. These increases widened the unfavourable gap between aid to adults – for example, the blind, disabled and elderly – and aid given to women and children (Miller, 1990). On the whole, though, the oil crisis and economic recession increased the number of claimants, as did demographic changes which included an increasingly elderly population. The US welfare system, which was not universal, came under criticism, and there were pressures to reduce public expenditure. Disillusionment with the 'Great Society' programmes opened the way for a new brand of politics. In the United States, as in Britain, the economic crisis of the 1970s provided the space for 'new' political and economic ideas to be taken seriously, leading to the election of a New Right administration committed to rolling back the state and reducing expenditure on social welfare.

Conclusion

The New Right ideology of the family is not new, nor is it in opposition to the image of the family held by the architects of the welfare state. What may be new is that it casts doubt on the proposition that state welfare policies can help sustain and support the family, arguing that welfare policies have in practice undermined and endangered it. The moral New Right therefore attack the welfare state for having imperiled the stability of the family and family life. This articulates with the economic New Right's attack on welfare spending as undermining the individual's right to decide how to provide for one's self and one's family. We shall argue, however, that attacks on the welfare state actually undermine the ability of families to provide for themselves, as well as attacking the limited rights of married women.

3

The Pro-Family Movement in Britain and the United States

Introduction

In the earlier chapters we have situated the rise of the New Right in Britain and the United States in the context of social, economic and political changes that have occurred since World War Two. We have pointed out that New Right ideology articulates elements of classical political economy with elements of conservatism. Those concerned with the economic New Right have mainly been concerned to examine the economic policies of Thatcher and Reagan.

As we have pointed out, the moral New Right has been concerned with the need for state action to monitor and reinforce traditional moral values and especially those associated with the patriarchal nuclear family. While not all those who stress what they see as the moral decay of modern society are Christians, Christians form the most vocal element. In the United States the main group politically active in pushing for state policies in 'moral' areas is the Christian New Right, consisting primarily of fundamentalist Protestant but also including other Christian groups such as the Roman Catholic Church and the Mormons. Similarly, in Britain those most vocal on moral issues are self-identified Christians – for example, members of the Conservative Family Campaign and the Festival of Light. Central to their concern with 'moral' issues is the family – specifically the heterosexual patriarchal family – which they see as being under threat from a decline in traditional morality and from state policies and especially welfare measures.

The Pro-Family Movement

Pro-family movements have developed in both Britain and the United States since the 1970s. These are movements with a political agenda, campaigning for the legislative changes which will remoralise society and support the privatised, patriarchal nuclear family. In both countries, administrations were in power in the 1980s which expressed commitment to the New Right pro-family ideas – Ronald Reagan in the United States and Margaret Thatcher in Great Britain. In Chapters 6 and 7 we shall be examining the extent to which Thatcher and Reagan have supported the pro-family movement with action as opposed to words and the extent to which governmental policies have benefited families more generally. In the rest of this chapter we propose to look at the origins of the movement in both countries and to explain how these pro-family issues appeared on the political agenda.

The aims of the pro-family movement in Britain and the United States are similar: they want to influence the political decision-makers so that policies are implemented which in their view will re-moralise society.

> Thus the pro-family movement is a broad-based coalition of social con-servatives who recognise the value of the person, the importance of the family, the rights and responsibilities of parents and the importance of restructuring government so that there can be personal freedom. (Gasper, 1981, p. 64)

However, as we have indicated above, the pro-family movement is concerned mainly with what it perceives as the moral decay of society, seeing most social ills as resulting from the breakdown of the family. Consequently the pro-family groups are concerned about a wide range of moral and economic issues. Members of the movement in both Britain and the United States are not just social conservatives; they also tend to be right-wing on a whole range of issues, including the economy and foreign policy.

> Abortion is only one of many issues. The whole picture includes drug abuse, alienation of youth, disrespect for authority, religious decline, decay of family structure, destruction of traditional education, revolution on the campus, racial strife, undermining of law enforce-ment and the judicial system, increase in homosexuality and perversion, inflation, repudiation of our currency, registration and confiscation of firearms, no-win wars, destruction of national pride and prestige, deliberate loss of the United States' military superiority and economic strength, planned and fabricated shortages of fuel and food leading to rationing and increasing control over the American people ... to fight abortion without understanding and fighting the total conspiracy is to ensure certain and total defeat. (John Grady, 'MD Abortion Yes or No?', American Public Opinion pamphlet quoted in Gordon and Hunter, 1977, p. 4)

In both Britain and the United States the pro-family movement can be seen as an integral part of the New Right, sharing the economic and foreign policy objectives as well as expressing specific moral priorities that received little or no attention in other New Right writing.

While the ideologies of the movement are the same in both countries, there are many clear differences. In Britain the pro-family movement has been small, has had little distinct media exposure and is little known. However, the New Right in Britain has been identified largely with the Conservative administration of Mrs Thatcher, who herself expresses pro-family views, as did key figures in her government. In the United States the New Right is a political movement separate from any political party. However, it has tended to campaign for right-wing Republicans, and Ronald Reagan's election as president was seen as a victory for the Moral Right. The leaders of the New Right in America explicitly set out to organise and revitalise the pro-family single-issue movement and to broaden its popular base in the late 1970s. The pro-family movement in the United States is thus a well organised and broadly based movement co-ordinating a number of single-issue organisations.

The Rise of the Pro-Family Movement in the United States

In the United States the pro-family movement developed out of an alliance of political, religious, anti-feminist and pro-life (anti-abortion) groups. This alliance was organised by the leaders of the self-styled New Right as part of a deliberate strategy for gaining popular appeal for their right-wing position, so that between 1977 and 1980 they developed a 'pro-family' lobby as one of the major organisational and policy strategies of the New Right. They explicitly set out to emphasise causes like busing, pornography, education, traditional biblical moral values and abortion because these were seen as issues that would win electoral support for their political agenda. Thus, as Paul Weyrich, director of the right-wing Committee for the Survival of a Free Congress, explained: 'social issues, at least for the present, fill the bill' (quoted in Cromartie and Newhaus, 1987, p. 79).

The leadership of the New Right has its roots in old right political organisations, such as the John Birch Society and the conservative wing of the Republican Party. Many of the leading figures in the New Right were activists in the Barry Goldwater campaign of the 1960s, an unsuccessful attempt to secure a Republican nomination for an extreme right-wing candidate for president. As a tight extra-party nexus of consistent political activity the New Right dates from 1974 when it was formed by four men: Richard Viguerie, Paul Weyrich, Howard Phillips and John 'Terry' Dolan. Paul Weyrich used his direct mail organisation to raise substantial funds for the New Right and to target particular populations with these ideas. The money went towards political action committees – organisations that campaigned in general elections but were not directly committed to any candidate. Paul Weyrich was the political strategist – he founded the Heritage Foundation (a New Right think tank) and many other New Right pressure groups. Terry Dolan founded the National Conservative Political Action Committee in 1975, the largest Political Action Committee (PAC) which set out to target for defeat or victory individual politicians standing for election. He was also active in other New Right organisations.

Another source of New Right support came from the local campaigns over specific issues which had been taking place over a longer period. Hence, for example, in some areas the attempts to desegregate schools and educate black and white children together by busing children from their neighbourhoods to different schools had been opposed by some white parents in some areas. This incipiently racist campaign was seized upon by the New Right and translated into a demand for parents to control their children's education. Other local campaigns included the campaign to retain prayers in schools and the control of school textbooks by parents who wanted no reference to birth control, sex or alternative family forms included. In some areas this included the rejection of the teaching of Darwin and evolutionary theories in favour of biblical ideas of creation. These activities also included campaigns against particular television programmes for their sexual content and local campaigns against abortion clinics which sometimes included burning them down. Howard Phillips concerned himself with mobilising locally based activists. He organised the Conservative Caucuses in 1975, which took part in local conservative campaigns and helped mobilise people who might not otherwise be politically active – for example, those involved in single issue groups such as the campaign for school prayers, for control of school textbooks, busing and so on.

In the late 1970s these and some other conservatives under Weyrich's guidelines set out to incorporate single-issue groups already in existence into a 'pro-family' movement. The Liberty Court group meeting from 1979 became the co-ordinating council for the pro-family movement. The main single-issue groups which they targeted were the anti-Equal Rights Amendment, anti-abortion, anti-busing, anti-pornography and other right wing moral family groups. Fundamentalist Protestants were also targeted, especially after the founding in the late 1970s of the Moral Majority by Jerry Falwell.

The incorporation of the fundamentalist Christians into the New Right was part of a deliberate strategy of broadening the conservative agenda to include popular moral issues. Until the 1970s fundamentalist Christians had rejected any involvement in politics, but they had become increasingly concerned over what they saw as the abandonment of absolute moral, Christian values in the United States and the rise of what they saw as an alternative religion: 'secular humanism'. Specific issues included the Supreme Court ruling that prayers or Bible readings in public (state) schools were unconstitutional, legislation for abortion, legalisation of gay, black and women's rights, as well as the increase in divorce and single parent families. By 1976 leading fundamentalist Christians were beginning to be politically active and many supported Jimmy Carter who identified himself as a fundamentalist during the 1976 Presidential campaign. Although Carter proved *not* to support the Christian New Right agenda, the fundamentalist leaders continued their political activities. The New Right leaders set out to incorporate the fundamentalist Protestants into a broad New Right political coalition in order to form the nucleus of the Christian New Right. They appointed a fundamentalist Protestant as the field director of the Conservative Caucuses, and in 1978 (an election year) planned an alliance to bring together the political New Right, the Protestant fundamentalists and the Catholic right-to-lifers (those campaigning against abortion). They adopted abortion as a key unifying issue. The New Right leadership from the late 1970s saw abortion as an issue that they could actively campaign on and organise. They viewed abortion as a consequence of sexual promiscuity and a humanist climate which placed individual moral decisions above those of the church. Furthermore, it was seen as a central civil right won by feminists. For the New Right the campaign against abortion formed the crux of its attempts to reverse the civil rights won by women and was part of a wider attack on feminism. While the New Right opposition to abortion is not based on the same moral criteria as that of the Roman Catholic Church, it set out to recruit anti-abortion Roman Catholics as well as bring other single issue groups underneath its umbrella. Fundamentalist leaders began to identify themselves with this movement and to argue that the religious New Right held a dominant position in this new conservative coalition.

The leaders of the New Right decided that it was necessary to develop a comprehensive organisation to co-ordinate the Christian New Right. This organisation was to be active in recruiting Americans to the moral agenda of the New Right, to act as a political lobby on moral issues and to raise funds for their activities. In 1979, Richard Viguerie, Paul Weyrich, Ed McAteer and others held a meeting to which Robert Bellings of the National Christian Action Coalition invited Jerry Falwell. They discussed with Falwell their shared opposition to legalised abortion and pornography and their hopes of influencing the 1980 Republican platform. At this meeting it was agreed that there was a 'moral majority' of Americans who shared their views on these 'moral' issues but whose views were being shut out by the liberals. They agreed to establish an organisation under the leadership of Falwell to spearhead a variety of Christian groups that would be politically active on these issues. They decided to call this organisation the Moral Majority. Falwell wanted the Moral Majority to be an ecumenical body made up of politically active Catholics, Jews, Protestants, Mormons and fundamentalists who shared the goal of making the United States a 'moral society' (Liberman, 1983, p.67). With the help of the New Right leaders Falwell put together a board of directors and founded three separate organisations: the Moral Majority Foundation, Moral Majority Inc. to act as a political lobby, and the Moral Majority Action Committee to use funds for political candidates.

These groups came together to create a new political coalition. The basis for recruitment may have been pro-family politics, but those recruited shared the commitment to capitalism and the free enterprise economy of the political leaders of the New Right – indeed, the fundamentalist Protestants were advocating a Christian basis for capitalism.

> The free enterprise system is clearly outlined in the Book of Proverbs in the Bible. Jesus Christ made it clear that the work ethic was a part of the plan for man. Ownership of property is biblical. Competition in business is biblical. Ambitious and successful business management is clearly outlined as a part of God's plan for His people. (Falwell, 1980)

The influence of the fundamentalist Christians in the US is strengthened by the use of TV and radio evangelism. The 'Electric Church', as it has become known, is a key element in the pro-family movement organising the New Right Christian movement. Televangelism is often seen as the single most important factor in the rise of the Christian New Right (Diamond, 1989). According to Diamond, by 1987 it was a billion dollar a year industry with more than 1,000 full-time Christian Radio stations and more than 200 full-time television stations. Originally begun as part of the churches' missionary work, by the 1980s religious broadcasting was a key element in increasing support for the Christian New Right in the United States itself. A number of television stations and specific programmes were seen to attract relatively large audiences. One programme – the '700 Club' on the Christian Broadcasting Network – was put out as a current affairs programme hosted by Pat Robinson (an American televangelist). While retaining the current affairs format, it consistently put across Christian New Right views on all the major political issues. There is, however, considerable controversy both as to size of audience and the impact of the Christian New Right televangelism (Diamond, 1989; Bruce, 1990). What is certain is that the effort put into televangelism by the Christian New Right demonstrates its determined attempt to win popular support for its political agenda. It has succeeded in attracting large enough audiences so that Christian New Right views have been consistently put across to a large segment of the public.

Two other key groups incorporated into the New Right 'pro-family' movement were the Stop Equal Rights Amendment (Stop-ERA) campaign, led by Phyllis Schlaffly and founded in 1972, and elements of the powerful anti-abortion lobby. These organisations provided a vehicle for the New Right to develop a mass base of support around various pro-family, pro-life, pro-moral and pro-American issues, with the family as the keystone.

The Stop-ERA, organised by Phyllis Schlaffly and her Eagle Forum Newsletter, was a single-issue organisation, mainly of middle class, middle-aged housewives mobilised around the issue of preventing the amendment to the constitution which would remove sexual discrimination. The ERA stated that 'Equality of Rights under the law shall not be denied or abridged by the United States or any state or any county on account of sex.' If ratified, it was suggested, the amendment would remove the rights of wives to economic support from their husbands, the right of exclusion of women from military service and so on. However, it was fundamentally an anti-feminist movement concerned with campaigning for protection for married women on the basis of the need for them to carry out their traditional role in the family for the sakes of their children, their husbands and the nation as a whole. Phyllis Schlaffly (who had been active for many years in right-wing political campaigns) argued for women to retain their traditional roles as wives and mothers and organised women to demonstrate their opposition to the ERA.

> The state conference in International Women's Year has been a big revelation to God-fearing, pro-family women as to what the women's liberation movement is all about. All over the country, women are rising up and saying 'No' to the demands of the libs for Federal control to replace family responsibility. (Phyllis Schlaffly, Eagle Forum, August 1977)

While the moral New Right believe that it is women's role to be subservient to men, to prioritise the care of their husbands and children, pro-family women have also been organised to fight for traditional family values. This kind of political activity is justified because it is seen as serving the interests of motherhood and children, not the selfish interests of individual women.

> Everything the Proverbs 31 woman did was for her family, her children, her husband, her home or her community. There is nothing in these issues about her rights or her own selfish decisions ... Men are geared towards action and are the first to strike whereas women plan strategy. (interview with Beverley Le Haye in *New Wine* quoted by Diamond, 1989, p.105)

The selective use of biblical sources is illustrated in the fact that Proverbs 31 also argues for the rights of the poor and needy.

Phyllis Schlaffly and Beverley Le Haye (wife of a Christian New Right leader and founder of 'Concerned Women for America') have both argued that women's primary responsibility is in the domestic sphere. Nonetheless, they have founded organisations that have attracted large numbers of pro-family women to help fight the Equal Rights Amendment Campaign and to campaign on such issues as abortion, pornography and school textbooks. Schlaffly is generally seen as being primarily responsible for organising successful opposition to ERA, while Le Haye was chosen, because of her position in 'Concerned Women for America', as a representative women's leader to testify at the Senate hearing on the nomination of Judge Bork to the Supreme Court in 1987.

The pro-life (anti abortion) movement in the United States was originally organised by the Catholic Church in about 1970, and it gained momentum after the Supreme Court Decision in Roe v. Wade which, in 1973, legalised abortion in the first trimestre. Not all of those opposed to abortion are right wing in their views. Nevertheless, opposition to abortion has been a key element in New Right activism and a basis for recruitment to New Right ideas and causes more generally.

The specific triggers for the formation of the pro-family movement in the United States seems to have been the International Women's Year Conferences in 1977 following President Jimmy Carter's announcement in 1976 that he was going to organise a White House Conference on Families. The International Women's Year Conference motivated a number of right-wing women's groups to formulate opposition to feminism, especially what they saw as the anti-family element. Explicitly, what they claimed was that large numbers of feminists – and, worse still, lesbians – were active at these events. At the same time, moral conservatives were opposed to Jimmy Carter's vision of the role of government in supporting and sustaining families and the broad definition of the family implicit in the way the conference was being organised. The New Right, in opposition, set out to demonstrate that there was only *the* family, not a variety of family forms. It maintained that there was a need to reinstate traditional moral values and that the government should stop interfering with the family.

The New Right leadership then set out to build on this base and to organise a social movement as a backlash. They sought to mobilise and co-ordinate the energy of the social movements in the service of conservative electoral politics. Thus, Weyrich has suggested that 'the major impact of family issues has been to elect Republican candidates' (Weyrich, 1983, p. 18)

The 'pro-family' movement was organised as a strategy of the New Right to win electoral success. From 1978, sexual and moral family issues became key elements in the New Right's electoral strategy – both for the candidates it supported and for those it opposed. This is not to suggest that the New Right leaders did not share these moral beliefs with those they organised, but that it was only one element in their broader commitment to right-wing policies. Thus, a Moral Majority leader in 1980 was reported as saying:

> It was the social issues that got us this far and that's what will take us into the future. We never really were until we began stressing issues like busing, abortion, school prayers and gun control. We talked about the sanctity of free enterprise, about the communist onslaught until we were blue in the face. But we didn't start winning majorities in the elections until we got down to gut level issues. (quoted in Davis, p. 2)

The election of Ronald Reagan to office in 1980 was seen as a considerable victory by the moral New Right. Throughout the 1980s the New Right was active in publicising its moral agenda and in election campaigns supporting right-wing Republicans. It also targeted politicians who it believed held the wrong moral values and actually tried to get them out of office by drawing up 'moral report cards'. How successful they have been in achieving their political goals is disputed (see Bruce, 1990; Jorstad, 1987). On balance they probably made little difference to the outcome of elections. However, they were successful in keeping the moral agenda alive in the United States throughout the 1980s.

The Pro-Family Movement in Britain

In Britain the New Right has been seen as virtually synonymous with the Conservative Administration under Margaret Thatcher's leadership. However, there is a moral New Right in Britain too, albeit not organised in the same way as the United States New Right with fundamentalist televised revival meetings to propagate the message and single-issue right-wing groups to be targeted. Nevertheless, there are groups and individuals in Britain who have emphasised that the root cause of Britain's economic and military decline as a nation is moral decline – the permissive society. These include Conservative Party members and ministers including Margaret Thatcher, right-wing 'think tanks' (most notably the Social Affairs Unit), New Right academics and individuals such as Victoria Gillick who led the campaign to prevent girls under 16 being given contraceptive advice by doctors without their parents' permission, elements within the Freedom Association, the Festival of Light and Mary Whitehouse's National Viewers and Listeners Association. Apart from those in government, many of the moral New Right themselves are in influential positions – for example, James Anderton, Chief Constable of Greater Manchester, who suggested that the breakdown of family morality was the cause of 'the highest ever rates of divorce, truancy, violence, vandalism in schools, drug abuse, alcoholism and terrorism.' (quoted in the *Manchester Evening News*, 3 March 1978).

The movement in Britain in the 1970s, organised as a backlash against the 'permissive society' and against left liberal influences, was mainly focused on two organisations : the National Viewers and Listeners Association (founded by Mary Whitehouse in 1965 and concerned with moral issues such as violence and sex in the media), and CARE (formerly Festival of Light, founded by Lord Longford, and mainly an anti-pornography organisation). These organisations along with the anti-abortion movements are not politically aligned and there has been no attempt to organise them or their members into a politically active 'pro-family' movement.

Families Need Fathers, a more explicitly 'pro-family' group, was founded in 1974. Its major concern was with what it saw as the marginalisation of divorced fathers. It argued that fathers should be given joint custody of their children and not seen just as joint financial providers. However, the group was basically opposed to divorce, blamed women's liberation for what it saw as the increasingly acceptable view that families do not need fathers and wanted to revive the authority of fatherhood which the group perceived as having been eroded.

Concern about the decline of the family and the view that this was the cause of many social and moral problems, linked explicitly with an attack on welfare spending, came onto the public agenda in the 1970s in the speeches of a number of influential Conservative politicians. In 1972 Keith Joseph, then UK Minister of Health and Social Security in the Conservative Administration, made his now famous 'cycles of deprivation' speech in which he argued that poor parenting resulted in the children of the poor remaining in poverty throughout their lives. In 1974 his ministry allocated £500,000 to the Social Science Research Council to fund academic research into cycles of deprivation. In the same year he founded the Centre for Policy Studies which has become a New Right think tank, contributing especially to debates on social policy issues. On 19 October 1974 in Birmingham, Sir Keith made a speech that clearly set down New Right thinking on the family:

> The socialist method would take away from the family and its members the responsibility which gave it cohesion. Parents are being divested of their duty to provide for their family economically, of their responsibility for education, health, upbringing, morality, advice and guidance, of saving for old age, for housing. When you take away responsibility from people you make them irresponsible. (Quoted in Raison, 1990, p. 90)

He argued that there was a connection between the decline in the family, welfare spending and social problems:

> Real incomes per head have risen beyond what anyone dreamed of a generation back, so have education budgets and welfare budgets, so also have delinquency, truancy, vandalism, hooliganism, illiteracy, decline in educational standards ... Teenage pregnancies are rising, so are drunkenness, sexual offences and crimes of sadism. For the first time in a century and a half, since the great Tory Reformer Robert Peel set up the Metropolitan Police, areas of our cities are becoming unsafe for peaceful citizens by night and even some by day. (Quoted in Raison, 1990, p. 90)

He goes on to suggest that a major 'problem' is poor single (mother) parent families:

> They are unlikely to be able to give children the stable emotional background, the consistent combinations of love and firmness which are more important than riches. They are producing problem children, the future unmarried mothers, delinquents, denizens of our borstals ... (quoted in Raison 1990, p.91)

Also in 1975, Ronald Bell, then Tory MP for Beaconsfield, said in a debate on the House of Commons Private Members Bill for Battered Wives that:

> I believe that a good deal of juvenile delinquency in the two generations since the end of the War has been accounted for by the weakening position of parents in the home, by legislation and by social work and even by such well-meaning bodies as the National Society for the Prevention of Cruelty to Children – I believe this is in large

measure due to the weakening of the position of the father in particular in the home. (Hansard, 11 July 1975 (c) 988, quoted in Smart, 1984)

Sir Keith Joseph was an important adviser and friend of Mrs Thatcher, and in 1975 she appointed him to chair an advisory committee on policy to report to the Shadow Cabinet. The brief for the committee particularly stated the need to consider the family. In 'Notes towards a Definition of a Policy' it was argued that unmitigated damage had been done to the strength of the family by policies such as urban redevelopment, the growing dependency on two incomes, too much television and too easy divorce and increasing numbers of single-parent families. It was argued that this damage had resulted in an increase in hooliganism, truancy, alcoholism, child abuse and criminality. It concluded that there was a need to find ways to rebuild family life and encourage families to take responsibility for their own members by reducing dependency on the state.

Leading Conservative politicians, including the newly elected leader Mrs Thatcher, increasingly made speeches supporting these views. By the time of the 1979 General Election the Conservative Party was arguing that it was the 'party of the family' – stressing the need for the patriarchal nuclear family to be supported, sustained and even returned to is place as the basic building block of the nation.

However, the major effort to develop a pro-family movement in Britain has come from the Conservative Family Campaign led by Graham Webster-Gardiner – a pressure group within the Conservative Party stressing the importance of moral and pro-family issues. It is explicitly tied to the Conservative Party and strongly supports that party while being critical of the ways it has dealt with moral and family issues while in power. The Conservative Family Campaign was formed in 1986 with the aim of remoralising the nation's life through the restoration of the traditional patriarchal family and a revival of fundamental Christian values. While it does not have the mass base of the US pro-family movement it is powerful within the Conservative Party, receiving support from a number of Conservative MPs and Members of the House of Lords at the time including: David Amess, Sir Bernard Braine, Viscount Buckmaster, Lady Colman, Baroness Cox, Harry Greenway, Peter Griffiths, Gerry Neale, Dame Jill Knight, Christopher Monckton, Ivor Stanbrook and Ann Winterton.

The Politics of the Pro-Family Movement

In Chapters 7 and 8 we intend to assess the ways in which the moral New Right have influenced public policy and the extent to which

Thatcher and Reagan can be said to have headed 'pro-family' administrations. We explore the ways in which the New Right moved from putting issues on the agenda to formulating policy objectives and the extent to which these policies have been realised. In the rest of this chapter we examine the key issues of the 'pro-family' movement and the political reforms implicitly or explicitly advocated.

We have already stressed that the 'pro-family' movement is concerned with sustaining the patriarchal nuclear family as the norm and that it is vigorous in its attack on welfarism, divorce, abortion and sexual deviancy. It is also anti-feminist and racist. The key areas in which it advocates political reform arise from these issues.

The 'pro-family' movement is a reaction to a perceived threat to the American or British way of life . Central to this image of life is the stable, patriarchal nuclear family – a family in which women are dependent on their husbands and parents responsible for their children. This means that in addition to more general issues such as welfare, divorce and abortion, more specific issues such as parental rights in education have been of concern to the 'moral' New Right. The issues that have been taken up and the policies that have been advocated are remarkably similar in both countries, although the exact form they take differs slightly. However, they all centre on the issue of the family and Christian morality.

The key issues are those of the role of men and women in the family, sexuality, parental control over children, and the debilitating effects of the welfare state. In terms of the role of men and women in the family the moral New Right are clear that men's role is as head of the family and economic provider; women's role is as the home-maker and carer for children. Given this, they are opposed to abortion because it gives women control over their own sexuality and frees men from having to take responsibility for their children. They are also opposed to contraception because it makes sex possible without having children – sex for enjoyment and recreation, not pro-creation – but more importantly because it endangers the family and family life. Women having paid employment outside of the home is also seen to endanger the stability of the family and of the nation. Wives' and children's dependence on the male bread-winner controls men, but it also controls women by making them economically dependent. Women who have paid employment not only fail to perform their familial duties but also develop independence which can result in divorce – a threat to the stability of the family unit. Thus the moral New Right see state intervention in family life – through the legalisation of abortion, through taking children into care and equal opportunities legislation – as endangering (or indeed already having destroyed) the stable family unit.

The state also endangers the stability of the family when it takes on responsibility for the care and socialisation of children by taking them away from the original family and into care. The father should be seen as the head of the family, as the moral leader of his wife and children. Parents have the responsibility of teaching their children morals and forming their characters. Thus, they argue that the state should not intervene in the family because it challenges the position of the husband/father as head of family. Schools should support parents and their roles, not undermine them, and parents should be able to choose which school their children shall attend. In the United States this set of views has been expressed in attitudes to busing (children being sent to schools at a distance from their home to achieve racially-mixed schools). Busing, it is argued, means that children do not go to a local school and therefore that the local community (parents) do not work with teachers in educating children. In Britain it has been expressed more explicitly in terms of parental choice but, as with busing in the United States, has taken on racist and cultural overtones when parents have objected to their children going to schools where there is a high percentage of British Asian children. Thus the article by the Bradford headmaster Ray Honeyford which appeared in the *Salisbury Review* (1984) and received much publicity argued that the needs of Asian children were 'swamping' those of white children. In the United States there have also been two other key issues – prayers in school and textbooks. The moral New Right have supported and organised groups which have argued for Christian values to be taught in schools and the censoring of textbooks that teach secular humanism – that man [sic] makes his own destiny as opposed to seeing it as a product of God's divine ordinance. In Britain there have been debates surrounding religious education in schools, with the moral New Right arguing that Christianity should be the main religion taught. They were influential in retaining Religious Education as a compulsory subject when the National Curriculum was introduced. The Amendment by Baroness Cox to the 1988 Education Reform Act is similarly illustrative of this in its retention of Christian worship in schools. In both countries the moral New Right has been opposed to sex education in schools and has argued that it should be taught within a Christian context that sets absolute moral values.

In Britain and the United States the attacks by the New Right on sexual promiscuity and what they see as sexual permissiveness have gone further than just criticising sex education in schools. They have attacked prostitution, pornography, and homosexuality. All are seen as threatening and undermining the nuclear family. Homophobia – the antagonism towards homosexuality – has been heightened by the moral panic around AIDS; AIDS has been portrayed by the moral

New Right as a gay plague and a judgement from God. Hence James Anderton, Chief Constable of Greater Manchester, has characterised homosexuals suffering from AIDS as 'stewing in a moral stew of their own making'. The implication is that they deserve to die a slow and painful death because of their moral corruption. The moral New Right want the reform of what they see as permissive legislation.

Finally, both in Britain and the United States the New Right have attacked welfarism, which they argue undermines the family. High welfare spending forces women to go out to work to maintain the standard of living of the family, which in turn disrupts family life.

> From the mid-1970s on it was necessary for women to enter the work force, not because they necessarily wanted to but because they were forced to [due to deficit spending on account of welfare programmes] ... Thirty-five million children under school age are being dumped into day-care centres. That's a lot of heady freedom to a fourteen or fifteen year old who comes home who knows that his Dad won't be home 'til later and his mother won't be home so he's got his girlfriend with him and why not. I mean after all, a little grass here, a little sex there, six hundred thousand teenage pregnancies last year – what's happening? Well, the mothers aren't home. (Pat Robinson, 'The Family and the Law' speech presented at the Family Forum 11 Conference, Washington D.C., 27 July, 1982)

More importantly, as Gilder and Murray argue (see Chapter 3), welfare payments help to encourage and maintain single-parent households – most notably, female-headed ones. These deviant family forms undermine the stability of society and also fail to provide children with adequate role models.

Given the generally anti-women stance of the New Right which we have described, it may seem surprising that aspects of their pro-family politics appeal to many women in America and Britain. Indeed, Klatch has argued (1987) that even within the New Right there are two distinct groups of women – those who are pro-individual and are concerned with the individual success of women, and those that are 'pro-family' or concerned with the subordination of women to the needs of family. Thus, for example, Edwina Currie calls herself a feminist and while a junior Health Minister did introduce reforms aimed at improving women's health, such as breast cancer screening. Mrs Thatcher has argued that it is mothers rather than women generally who should stay at home (although she exempts herself because she could afford a nanny!) and there is some confusion in moral New Right thinking as to whether mothers should be seen as individuals or as having a biological destiny (see Lawrence Mead in Chapter 5). Furthermore, many middle-aged women who have stayed at home and cared for their husbands and children do feel threatened by changes – specifically, that they will be divorced by their husbands and left without support and unable to find good employment because of their age and lack of marketable skills. These fears are real.

Conclusions

There are considerable similarities between the 'pro-family' movements in Britain and the US. They share a common diagnosis of the cause of economic and political decline of the nation, they have a common definition of the family, and the policies they advocate are essentially similar. They propose policy changes that will reverse a wide array of liberal and progressive reforms enacted since World War Two. The moral New Right is more organised as a social movement in the United States, but the appeal to the moral arguments of the New Right is also evident in Britain. In both countries the popular appeal of family life and campaigns on particular moral issues are used to recruit people to New Right political ideology as a whole. The New Right uses moral and family issues as a populist strategy to recruit people to its ideological position. As Ehrenreich (1987) points out with respect to the US (and we would argue it is equally applicable to the UK):

> ... the American New Right does offer an alternative view to endless disruption and aimless individualism of bourgeois society. It is a view of the future in which people will live in stable families within stable communities and will work hard and be sober and chaste. (p.102)

4

British New Right Intellectuals and the Family: Roger Scruton and Ferdinand Mount

So far we have described some of the ideas of the Moral Right and their origins. These ideas have to some extent been developed by right wing academics, 'think tanks' and in the pages of journals by particular groups of intellectuals. With the coming to power of Thatcher in Britain there was a veritable flowering of New Right thinking, emanating from institutions such as the Adam Smith Institute, the Institute of Economic Affairs, and the Centre for Policy Studies. Their ideas are disseminated through the pages of learned journals such as the *Salisbury Review* and through weeklies and popular papers such as *The Spectator*, the *Daily Telegraph*, and even *The Times*. New Right columnists have had privileged access to the media, and the ideas of New Right intellectuals have been particularly influential and important given that the government in power is receptive to their arguments. There is much cross-fertilisation between British and US intellectuals: they invite each other to speak at conferences and to join 'think tanks' on both sides of the Atlantic and in other parts of the English-speaking world such as Australia, New Zealand and Canada.

Only a few British intellectuals have written on moral issues. Roger Scruton and Ferdinand Mount stand out as intellectuals who have considered the role of the family, with both of them attempting to justify and defend the patriarchal nuclear family. They seek to demonstrate that marriage and the heterosexual, patriarchal nuclear family are inevitable. Not only is this form of family to be seen as inevitable, but it is also the most desirable family form, without which human happiness and the social structure are threatened. While they are both arguing for the same end and are critical of many of the same things – such as feminism and sexual liberation – they are basing their arguments on very different philosophical premises and for this reason it is important to tackle each one separately. There are also other important differences between them. Ferdinand Mount writes within a radical libertarian framework, often using the vocabulary of the revolutionary left, while Roger Scruton comes more from the authoritarian strand within the New Right: he argues in defence of nation and submission to authority and tradition.

Roger Scruton and Sexual Desire

Roger Scruton is Professor of Philosophy at the University of London and a barrister. He is the author of a number of books, including *The Meaning of Conservatism,* and he used to be editor of the *Salisbury Review,* 'a journal of Conservative ideas', as it describes itself. He often presents his ideas – including many of those which emerged in his book *Sexual Desire* (1986) – in a popular form in his controversial column in *The Times*.

His elegantly written book *Sexual Desire* is a dense philosophical treatise in which he puts forward a celebration and justification of 'bourgeois' morality – a term traditionally vilified by left-wing intellectuals and artists alike so that it is usually seen as an insult. In this he claims to be defending old-fashioned virtues such as modesty, faithfulness and 'decency'. As rational and thinking human beings we inhabit an everyday reality which he terms the *Lebenswelt* – the world of rational contemplation and moral choice. This *Lebenswelt* is much shaped by the ideals of bourgeois morality. Bourgeois morality therefore consists of commonsense assumptions which in Scruton's theory attain a transcendent importance. The commonsense world, having been constructed through the daily actions and thoughts of the bourgeoisie, is embedded in real life situations and has acquired a solidity and meaningfulness through the product of rational contemplation over centuries. It is therefore better than the sorts of ideas which critical (that is, left-wing and de-constructionist) intellectuals would like to construct out of their latest, fashionable, ungrounded and unsubstantiated ideas. 'If the *Lebenswelt* is a bourgeois invention then we should praise and emulate the bourgeois mind, which is better fitted to perceive the human reality than the ordered consciousness of the "demystifying" critic' (p. 13).

He goes on to express the idea that the bourgeois heterosexual family is the product of this bourgeois morality which we need to defend. We need to defend it particularly against ideologues who would dissolve it and replace it with something else out of their own alienated imagination – their imagination being 'alienated' because they cannot accept the day-to-day conventions of life as it exists. Sexual liberation – which he sees alienated critical intellectuals as recommending – is simply a myth which would seek to subvert the family and offer nothing in its place (p.347). Sexuality and gender roles are thus inevitably tied into the nuclear heterosexual family and the institution of marriage through which it is established.

For Scruton this position is based upon a phenomenological concept of the integral 'person' who is a moral being and is the product of 'intentionality'. Sexual desire cannot be divorced from our moral personhood and our view of the other person as a unique moral entity. Hence, I do not desire you because you have large thighs and tight buttocks but because you are a person – but you may also have these attributes which I find attractive. It is because they are part of you that I find them so appealing. The reduction of people to things and parts is therefore obscene because their 'personhood' has been removed. Scruton thus criticises sexologists such as Kinsey or Masters and Johnson for reducing sex to a series of functions and localised reactions. However, he also criticises Foucault (the post-modernist author of three volumes on the history of sexuality) for arguing that sexuality is the creation of significance around arbitrary features which are historically created, for arguing in other words against 'essentialism' or the idea that sex roles exist in essence. Scruton argues instead that sexual desire is grounded in the *essential* difference between male and female and between different persons. Gender roles thus exist in essence – they are not arbitrary historical constructs as Foucault has maintained. Because these differences are a universal part of the human experience the interplay between them is always present and societies can institutionalise them in different ways which can be better or worse for human happiness and for the game of sexual desire. The corollary of this essential difference between the sexes is that heterosexuality is the natural and normal relationship between them and marriage institutionalises this heterosexual bond.

He argues, too, against feminists but, here he creates an opponent – the 'Kantian feminist' (not a term recognised by feminists but which appears to resemble liberal feminism) – who is a representation of only one kind of feminist position . The Kantian feminist, he claims, would wish to minimise the difference between the sexes, to set up an equality of people in which sex differences play no part – or only a minor part. He rejects this position because he sees the differences between the sexes as an inevitable part of the human condition and a product of our socialisation within our bodies. For women the experience of the body is associated with that of pregnancy and menstruation, but the awareness of the body extends from earliest childhood as we try to make sense of ourselves. Thus 'gender' is rooted in our physical sex but not reducible to it. This characterisation of feminism of course does not apply to some feminists, including radical feminists, who would, like Scruton, view the sexes as differentiated in their experiences and sense of identity. However, unlike Scruton, radical feminists would not see this as inevitably leading to union through the sexual act, but rather as a good reason for the sexes to stay apart because men are naturally aggressive and dominating toward women (Abbott and Wallace, 1990).

Scruton aims to show that romantic love was not an illicit product of courtly love invented by the troubadours in the Middle Ages – as some historians have argued – nor was it a product of the free individualism of the modern age, but that it has existed throughout history, and he uses classical texts to back this up. He is at great pains to demonstrate that romantic love was not classically only a product of illicit or adulterous relationships but has also existed within lasting unions between men and women. Indeed, Scruton sees the sexual act (by which he means sexual intercourse and penetration of the woman by the man) as the necessary way in which the genders are united, the way in which their physical animality are made one with their moral personhood. All else is foreplay or perversion (p.89). Again this vision of unity between the genders in the sexual act and the ultimate purpose of sexual activity and courtship being sexual intercourse is a masculine and heterosexist view of sexual relationships. It does not allow a broader and more variegated view of sexual relations, despite all the exotic examples which he cites. On this basis he condemns activities such as fetishism and pornography as obscene perversions because they remove the person from the sexual act. Sado-masochism and masturbation can be perversions if they replace the person with fetishised objects but they can also have more harmless manifestations which retain the idea of the person.

However, Scruton has more trouble with the idea of homosexuality. Homosexuality, as long as it does not take place with children, is the sexual desire between two mature 'persons' exercising moral choice, even though they are of the same sex. Therefore it should be assimilable with Scruton's model of acceptable sexual relations. However, here he resorts to the idea that most people are disgusted by the idea of homosexuality because it offends the principle of 'complementarity'. The concept of 'complementarity' which is introduced here is not philosophically justified but refers to the teachings of the Catholic Church – hardly the most useful source for trying to establish a *rational* basis for traditional morality. He has to confess himself stumped otherwise because he is really wanting to justify traditional morality rationally and his carefully argued philosophical schema does not help him on this, hence his careful circumlocutions:

> The correct position, I believe, is this: homosexuality is perhaps not in itself a perversion, although it may exist in perverted forms. But it is *significantly* different from heterosexuality, in a way that partly explains, even if it does not justify, the traditional judgement of homosexuality as a perversion. I say this with extreme tentativeness ... (p. 305)

What reasons does he give for this?

> The fact of sexual difference becomes ever less important as desire roams freely over the two sexual kinds. The idea of the moral indistinguishability of homosexual and heterosexual desire is made possible by the gradual evaporation of gender distinctions, and the construc-

tion of a new order of desire, in which what is sought in desire is not the complement, but the simulacrum of present feeling ... (p. 309)

This, he says, is surely wrong. But why should it be obscene and excite such disgust?

Is there anything in the homosexual act which is the *proper* object of obscene perception? A positive answer to that question must rely, I believe, on the strangeness of the the the other gender – on the fact that heterosexual arousal is arousal by something through and through other than oneself, and other as flesh. In the heterosexual act, it might be said, I move *from* my body *towards* the other, whose flesh is unknown to me; whilst in the homosexual act I remain locked within my body, narcissistically contemplating in the other an excitement that is the mirror of my own. (p. 310)

Therefore, he goes on, the disgust of most people at this relationship can be justifiably extended to all homosexual relationships, which are horrible because they take the form of sexual desire with someone too similar to oneself and which therefore do not pose the same challenges as relationships with the opposite sex.

This argument seems weak on two counts. First, there can be as many differences between people of the same sex as there are between sexes, so that the idea of complementarity and differences is not sustainable. Indeed, people tend to marry people rather similar to themselves in terms of age, social class, ethnicity. Secondly, the generalised disgust allegedly felt by most people is not a good enough reason to condemn homosexuality and is not sustainable in terms of his own philosophical argument. Many people feel disgust at the idea of fellatio and yet he sees this as a thoroughly healthy – and philosophically justified – activity. The idea of taking commonsense bourgeois morality as the basis of a 'natural' morality shows its flaws here. It means that Scruton can simply use popular prejudices as universal truths and is able to justify a homophobic culture. Because it exists it must be right; because it is right it exists.

Another problem is that he cannot explain – apart from vague references to the different ways in which we grow up in our bodies – the differences between males and females. In explaining the male homosexual's predatory and promiscuous behaviour as opposed to the more gentle and consensual activity of the lesbian he resorts to naturalistic assumptions – that males are 'naturally' predatory and females 'naturally' modest (p.309). In other words, the dominance and superiority of what he calls the 'vagrant' penis is encouraged by 'natural' female loyalty and hesitation: nothing to do with personhood, this – just a restatement of traditional patriarchal myths.

No justification is given for why the male desire should be conquering and the female one hesitant. This leads to a rather confusing and unconvincing description of lesbianism based upon a reading of the ancient Greek Sappho – that because women are unable by their nature to take the sexual initiative, lesbians must be reduced to a shadowy existence of hopes and prayers (p.308). Had he read something from the wealth of more recent lesbian literature he might have been able to give a more realistic picture of lesbianism. However, his view is obstructed by the masculine view of sex as polarised between assertiveness and passivity, dominance and submission.

Scruton attempts to deal with this masculine bias by arguing at the beginning that he is using the pronoun 'he' throughout in a gender neutral way – to refer to both sexes, except where the person must be a she. However, this reinforces rather than undermines the universality of the male gaze in his work. For example, the seducer is nearly always male, the seduced female; the prostitute female and the client male. 'The "pollution" of the prostitute is not that she gives herself for money, but that she gives herself to whom she hates and despises' (p. 341). He also argues that the prostitute 'pollutes' herself by divorcing sexuality from chastity: marriage is and should be based upon sexual repression. This serves to reinforce uncritically the assignation of women to a feminine role and in the case of prostitution to an exploited role, focusing on the prostitute (and the familiar moral condemnation of the prostitute) rather than the client who (as in real life) gets off virtually scot free. Even where Scruton attempts to talk about attraction with a masculine object it sounds peculiar and unconvincing. While he has attempted to demonstrate the universality of sexual desire and sexual difference by using examples from classical mythology and from all periods of history, he uses male authors describing their own desires (since these inevitably predominate) or female desires as evinced through the eyes of male authors. Indeed, as his 'evidence' he uses some male authors who are well known and avowed misogynists – such as Strindberg or Juvenal – but this passes without comment. Hence, the descriptions of female desires are mysterious and unconvincing – for example, the description of the Roman empress who it is alleged enjoyed erotic fulfilment by arranging for geese to nibble seeds from her belly and thighs in front of an audience, or the account of the female classical figure who fell in love with a bull. These classical sources are especially suspect because the original authors were trying to demonstrate the decadence of the late Roman Empire through the misbehaviour of womenfolk allowed to express their sexuality freely. This is female desire seen through male eyes and it would fail to convince most women as an erotic act. The use of a range of classical and literary sources also gives this writing an air of unreality since very few contemporary examples are used. Very occasionally a passage from a female author intrudes, but not enough to shift the overwhelming impression of sexual desire as seen through the male gaze. Indeed the only account of lesbian sex by a modern lesbian is dismissed as bad prose. Similarly accounts of beatings as being highly exciting for male participants is not convincing for female readers for whom sexual violence and violence by men generally has traditionally been something terrifying, a source of male power and used to oppress and control women.

On account of this male bias, the blatantly sexist and misleading passages from cited authors pass without comment. Furthermore, the issues associated with gender differences in sexual desire that would strike most women as being important and which need explanation – for example, why it is that a pornography industry has grown in order to satisfy mainly male demands, why rape and sexual harassment are characteristically male proclivities and why prostitutes are usually female and their clients usually male – are not addressed at all and there is no explanation for them in Scruton's scheme.

Although the early part of the book is an elaborate attempt to set up a phenomenological theory for sexuality which includes an explicit and detailed rejection of sociobiological reductionism, Scruton is unable to account for 'essential' sex differences using his own theory. Hence he needs to resort to naturalistic explanations of sexual difference in terms of men's 'natural' predatory instinct and need to dominate women sexually, which is justified by reference to a sort of sociobiological 'Just-So Story'. This is worth quoting at length because it is here that Scruton gets round the problem of explaining the sorts of sexual difference which manifest themselves in our society by simultaneously denying and accepting this mythological explanation:

> The man is active in the pursuit of women; he does not confine his attentions to one woman only, but moves on restlessly after new conquests, and attempts to exclude other men from enjoying their favours. Moreover, his jealousy has a peculiar focus. He is pained, not so much by the attempt by other men to help and support his woman, as by their attempt to unite with her sexually. Indeed, it is the thought of her copulating with another which causes him the greatest outrage ... At the same time, he has a disposition to provide for her, and to seek food and shelter that will facilitate the nourishment of his children.
>
> The woman is not active in the pursuit of men, but modest and retiring. She thereby guarantees that she can be obtained only at the cost of effort and determination, and so ensures that her genes will unite with the strongest available strain, thus furthering their chances of survival. Once possessed, she does her utmost to secure the services

of the man, and to bind him to her, so as to enjoy the fruits of his protection during the times ahead ... The disparity between the genetic requirements of man and woman is reflected also – according to the imaginary portrait I am offering – in the structure of male and female desire. The man will be attracted to those features in the woman which promise healthy offspring and easy childbirth. He will be moved by her youth, vitality and regular features; by her readiness for domestic life, and by her modesty. He will value chastity, and even virginity: the harbingers of his own genetic triumph. And he will try to win her by a display of strength and competence.

She, however, will respond to the man who promises the greatest protection to her offspring. She is impressed less by his youth than by his power. Everything that promises security is capable of arousing her affections, and even a far older man may excite her, provided there is, in his look, his smell, his conversation or his social manner, the necessary virtues of a father ... At the same time, she will not be indifferent to a man's physical character and – like him – will be turned away by evident deformities, and by the signs of intellectual or emotional decay ...

... Suppose, however, that such a picture – which I have presented in the broadest outline – were true to our biological condition, and to the psychological dispositions that are rooted in it. Would this not have the greatest imaginable implications for our ideas of gender? In particular, *would it not suggest that the traditional conception of gender, according to which men and women have different characters, different emotions, and different social and domestic roles, is neither biological accident nor a social superfluity?* (pp. 262–4, emphasis added)

The question is a rhetorical one, but Scruton answers it implicitly by referring to 'natural' and 'innate' differences between the sexes to describe sexual desire and the inevitability of patriarchy.

Of course, as feminists we could equally present other biologically based myths for the foundation of gender relations – for example the sexual dominance of the female of the species in selecting males as mates, and the limited sexual potential of the male who must recover his strength, could lead one to speculate that men have needed to compensate for their sexual inadequacy by political control. However, such speculation is pointless since we can use biology neither to prove nor disprove the inevitability of aspects of human society.

This rejection of sociobiology but simultaneous acceptance of this strange sexist Just-So Story as the foundation for gender differences can be explained in the following way. Scruton goes to great lengths to lay the foundations for understanding men and women as gendered subjects inhabiting a moral *Lebenswelt*. However, the movement from this to describing the inevitability of sexual domination by men and subordination on the part of women is far from convincing and not well established. This is where he needs help from sociobiology.

But it would be wrong to characterise Scruton as a crude biological reductionist (like, for example, George Gilder, whom we discuss later). His book is written precisely in order to argue for the construction of social life by intentional, moral persons. In the final chapter he introduces the idea of the 'sacred' as the thing of value in the social world which should be preserved and the 'polluted' and 'obscene' as something to be rejected. The social actors in the social world, whilst being born with a sex, self-consciously construct themselves through gender in different areas of social life. For Scruton the relationship between persons is extremely fraught, painful and difficult, particularly in the field of intimate relations where personal exposure is required. Hence people relate to each other through institutions – institutions like the church, education, marriage and the family. These institutions are socially constructed – and therefore not inevitable – but they represent the product of many centuries of ways of relating to one another and, he argues, are therefore like old pebbles worn smooth with much use. For this reason they are adapted for mediating human relationships most effectively. In other words, they are the best because they are the ones which have withstood the passage of time.

The institution of marriage has other advantages in rendering private the sexual act between men and women and therefore protecting this very fragile and fraught relationship. Furthermore, by denying sexual activity in other contexts – through fidelity, chastity, restraint – it makes the ritualised interplay of sexual desire all the more intense and erotic. What this appeal to tradition fails to address, however, is how that tradition is founded upon male interests in sexuality and private property rather than female ones, how the interests of one sex have historically held institutional power over those of the other.

Furthermore, this underplays class differences and the historical transformations which have taken place, and also the irrelevance of sexual desire for some sorts of unions – for example, the Victorian marriage where women were not supposed to feel erotic desire and the political marriage based upon the interests of the wider kin. The linking of sexual desire as a necessary adjunct of a freely chosen heterosexual couple union and the implication that this is the universal epitome of desirable living is also racist in its implications because it relegates other forms of domestic union – such as arranged marriages or multiple spouses – to the status of deviance or immorality. Nor is sexual desire an inevitable feature of many 'freely chosen' marriages. For women the economic necessity of remaining married may take priority over other disadvantages – such as incest and violence – irrespective of moral considerations and free will. The economic bonds of marriage are therefore ignored in Scruton's model or seen as 'reductionist' because most men are not in a position to have to worry about them. Hence the prostitute in Scruton's theory can be seen as someone who is morally reprehensible because she has sex with people she despises rather than being seen as someone who needs to earn money. Loving a murderer or a rapist is seen as morally contemptible by Scruton but may be an economic necessity for some women. The strange sexual antics described for some of the women in Scruton's book are only possible in a world where sexual desire for women is often subordinate to economic necessity.

However, Scruton does descend from the abstract stratosphere of moral philosophy with obscure and peculiar classical illustrations to make connections between sexual desire, the institution of marriage and private property today:

> It is a small step from the institution of marriage to that of private property. The exclusive erotic relation fights for its exclusive territory; for the right to close a door. Within that territory everything is 'shared', and since only what is privately owned can be privately shared, the sphere of marriage and of the family is one of private ownership. Moreover, ownership of the home (in the wide sense of 'tenure' as this concept has been developed in English law) is ownership of a stake in the means of production. (p. 360)

This connection is by no means obvious, however, since the meaning of privacy in relation to sexual desire does not rest upon material foundations in Scruton's argument until this point. Furthermore, English law did not until recently recognise the wife's share of the property nor are many marriages sharing ones since material inequalities exist within them. Once more Scruton has thrown us a red herring in order to use his philosophical exposure of 'truth' to support the patriarchal nuclear family. Unfortunately for him, this argument is not sustainable. Women do not necessarily get an equal share of private property and the patriarchal nuclear family does not guarantee sharing. There is no necessary connection between sharing one's body and sharing one's property.

To summarise the arguments against Scruton's view of sexual desire: first, he sees 'bourgeois morality' as a universal transcendent set of values which are grounded in popular common sense. This means that rather than setting up an alternative rational basis for sexual morality, it is merely tautological: what exists must be right and it is right because it exists and people believe in it. Secondly, he mistakes the male gaze – his own and that of the many male authors whom he cites – as being some sort of definitive and representative view of sexuality. In fact it represents female sexuality only in a distorted way. Thirdly, while philosophically rejecting the position of biological reductionism, he resorts to a sociobiological argument to explain what he sees as essential and natural differences in male and female sexuality which he cannot otherwise explain with the theory which he himself has constructed.

Ferdinand Mount – the Subversive Family

Ferdinand Mount is a journalist whose ideas on the family were influential because he was an adviser to Mrs Thatcher in the early 1980s through his post in the Central Policy Review Staff Policy Unit. Here we will only be examining his book *The Subversive Family*, published in 1982. Mount represents New Right ideas in some ways better than Scruton because he is arguing for a libertarian view of the family – that it will reassert itself as part of the spontaneous order if not interfered with by the state or the church and that it forms a natural defence for freedom and equality.

Mount, unlike Scruton, takes a more conventional approach to history using the work of the Cambridge Centre for Population Studies in an attempt to demonstrate that the nuclear family has always existed and is a natural unit for human fulfilment and happiness: 'Marriage and the family make other experience, both pleasant and unpleasant, seem a little tame and bloodless. And it is difficult to resist the conclusion that a way of living which is both so intense and so enduring must somehow come naturally to us, that is part of being human.' (p. 256)

In doing so, he seeks to explode various popular and academic myths (many of which have been exploded before in other ways), namely:

1. That the family is an historical freak. Mount seeks to demonstrate, using examples throughout history, that the nuclear family has always existed and persisted through time, that it is in fact universal:

    The sceptics make two points: first, the nuclear family is *universal*. Wherever more complicated forms exist, the nuclear family is always present as well. Second, in England and North-Western Europe, the nuclear family was the *standard* situation – a simple family living in its own house. (p.53)

2. That the nuclear family is unique to our society, and is not found in non-Western societies. To do this he attacks the early nineteenth-century anthropologists (who were already much discredited by the twentieth century). His argument is weak here

because no contemporary anthropologists would claim that the nuclear family exists nowhere else – nor would they claim that it existed universally! For example, a contemporary anthropologist, Felicity Edholm (1982), drawing upon a range of evidence, argues that the monogamous, patriarchal nuclear family is not universal. Moreover, although other social arrangements may appear to us to be similar to our own family form, in fact they hold very different beliefs about paternity, parenthood, gender roles and so on. Furthermore, she argues that the co-resident household is normally part of a wider set of kin relations through which many non-Western societies are organised. The nuclear households are seldom as isolated as those in the West.

3. That marriages were arranged by parents in the past. Mount uses historical evidence to argue that matches which did not involve property transfers depended upon free choice by partners and even in those which did, negotiations could founder on the non-compliance of the people to be betrothed.

4. That the idea of romance was invented by the Medieval troubadours and that it referred only to illicit and adulterous passion. This has been argued by historians of romantic love. Mount argues that this was a French myth and that in fact there is plenty of evidence of warm and sentimental feelings between betrothed and married partners of a more down-to-earth and Anglo-Saxon kind throughout history. But it should not be forgotten that marriages in non-capitalist and pre-capitalist societies could be based upon very different precepts – the acquisition of property or a livelihood were important in determining whether a person could marry at all as well as to whom.

5. That the love of children is quite recent because so many children died in the past, mothers were relatively indifferent to them. Mount refers to this argument put forward by historians Edward Shorter (1975) and Lawrence Stone (1977) to explain the relativity of maternal love and our views of childhood. They cite the large numbers of foundlings and abandoned babies as evidence, but Mount argues that these were simply a product of the economic privations which forced parents to give up their children. In fact they loved them just as much as parents today. However, in refuting this idea of the absence of maternal love, Mount goes on to reject the idea that children were treated in any different way in the past than they are today. In fact, other historians, including Aries (1965) have argued that we need to look at the way views and discourses about children have served to construct childhood differently at different periods of time. The purpose and function of children in societies where they were used as workers and as insurance against old age (and still are) is different from one where they are seen as having no economic function – regardless

of the quality of parental love. Also, the development of psychological and medical theories of childhood and the advent of universal education have similarly served to create a different experience of childhood than existed in the past (Rose, 1985). In rejecting the views of Shorter and Stone that parents did not love their children in the past it is not correct to claim – as Mount does – that they therefore saw their children in exactly the same way as we do.

6. That divorce is a recent phenomenon and associated with the breakdown of the family. Mount presents evidence to show that divorce was frequent and cheap in previous centuries and that it was only the increasing control by the church which sought to make it more difficult. Furthermore he argues there was usually provision for abandoned wives and children. However, whereas divorce may have been more easily obtained at other points in history, it was plainly not the case in nineteenth-century Britain where men could divorce women but women could not divorce men, and women abandoned by absconding husbands often ended up in the workhouse and constituted a major social problem. Even now, one major cause of poverty for women (and not for men) is divorce and single parenthood. Mount argues that nowadays the welfare state provides a 'safety net' which catches women and children as they fall out of marriage and provides for them. However, life on income support does not represent a very happy existence, so women still stay in unhappy marriages for economic support. Divorce is still not an easy way out of a disagreeable relationship for most women and it is unlikely that it ever was.

   Mount differs from the rest of the 'moral' New Right in arguing for the virtues of easy divorce; it is the moral New Right who above all have pointed to rising divorce rates as being evidence of the breakdown of the family and, leading from this, of society as a whole. Many of the moral New Right have argued for the tightening of divorce laws to make divorce more difficult and the removal of income support for single-parent families in order to provide economic discouragement (see Chapters 6 and 7).

7. That the church and state have always been supporters of the family. Mount's main argument here is against the church – and particularly the early church – in its rejection of the family in favour of a life wedded to the church. However, it is many centuries since this was the case, and for most periods of history it was more common for the church to attempt to control marriage and family life. Mount argues that the control of marriage and the family by the church or state is always the outcome of an historical struggle in which the family eventually wins against its enemies. The sequence runs as follows:

First, hostility and propaganda to devalue the family. The family is a source of trouble. It could distract apostles or potential apostles from following the new idea. The family is second-best, pedestrian, material, selfish. Alternative families are promoted – communes, party cadres, kibbutzim, monasteries.

Second, reluctant recognition of the strength of the family. Despite all official efforts to downgrade the family, to reduce its role and even to stamp it out, men and women obstinately continue not merely to mate and produce children but to insist on living in pairs together with their children, to develop strong affections for them and to place their family concerns above other obligations.

Third, collapse of efforts to promote the alternative pseudo-families ...

Fourth, a one-sided peace treaty is signed. The church or the state accepts the enduring importance of the family and grants it a place in the orthodox dogma or ideology ...

Fifth, history is rewritten to show that the church or the state *always* held this high conception of the family ...

Sixth, the family gradually manages to impose its own terms ... (pp. 3–4)

Hence, Mount is keen to argue that the natural family naturally reasserts itself. This is also very different from the views of many of the moral New Right who would see the church as the upholder of the family. Scruton, for example, sees the Roman Catholic Church as the guarantor of moral behaviour whereas Mount sees the Roman Catholic Church as even more of an enemy of the family than other variations of Christianity.

Mount argues that the state as well as the church has been the traditional enemy of the family. It would be true perhaps to say that the state had little interest in the family until recently except insofar as the legal system sought to safeguard the transmission of property. The family was considered a private realm over which the male head of household ruled. It is only recently, with the rise of the welfare state since the nineteenth century, that there has been much interest in the family, but this has mainly been in order to strengthen and reproduce it (as we argue in Chapters 5 and 6). Indeed, we would argue that the modern nuclear family is a product of various state interventions. For example, the creation of a universal education system at the end of the nineteenth century and extending into youth training programmes now creates children and young people as family dependants. The pension system and the age of retirement creates a category of elderly dependants. The interventions of concerned professionals such as health visitors and social workers were concerned to ensure proper standards of mothering and family care rather than to undermine the family (Abbott and Wallace, 1990).

8. That the family is threatened by the growth of alternative styles of living such as kibbutzim and communes. Mount's arguments here that these are usually short-lived alternatives which revert to nuclear family forms is based on many studies over the years of these alternative styles of living. However, we could argue that this is less to do with the natural resilience of the nuclear family as with the pervasiveness of familial ideology within contemporary capitalism. Furthermore, women were not always best served by these alternative styles of living which often simply replicated the traditional domestic division of labour on a larger and more institutionalised scale. Women were still doing the cleaning and childcare. To what extent did they actually offer an alternative to the nuclear family?

Therefore, Mount argues, the family has persisted throughout time. However, he makes greater claims for the family than this. He argues that it is in fact a *revolutionary* force: 'That is why I speak of the family's permanent revolution against the State, and the working-class family as the only truly revolutionary class' (p. 162). This is because the family resists authority, whatever form authority has taken over the centuries; for this reason, those in authority always hate the family. His main attack is against the church, which he argues has tried to eradicate the family in order to recruit disciples to 'higher callings' – that is, total commitment to the church. The family, being a selfish institution in which people are committed to each other and to providing for their children, must always weaken commitment to higher authorities and goals.

However, there is a sinister side to this attempt to secure the hearts and minds of followers – it is simply substituting a higher authority and is therefore always authoritarian and totalitarian. Mount argues that 'fear and distrust have always pervaded and distorted the Church's view of everything to do with marriage' (p.22) and particularly their view of sexuality. However, once they realised that the only way to control sexuality was to acknowledge marriage, they grudgingly acceded to this and then later tried to institutionalise 'Holy Matrimony' as a religious institution. The church also tried to control what went on inside marriage by encouraging its adherents to abjure 'sexual immoderation' and stick to purely routine procreation with as little sex as possible. In this way the church sought to incorporate marriage into its rituals and, by preventing divorce, attempted to control marriage.

However, most of these examples are taken from the early Roman Catholic Church. For many centuries now, the church has accommodated rather than opposed the family. How far can this argument be sustained given the long reign of the established church in Britain and its part in perpetuating monogamous nuclear families?

Another enemy of the family, according to Mount, is the state. He uses the example of the encouragement of bachelorhood amongst army officers so that they could have total allegiance to the state (there was no attempt in this case, however, to discourage sexual relations). According to Mount, the modern welfare state uses different tactics against the family – it sends in the caring professional:

> The family's most dangerous enemies may not turn out to be those who have openly declared war. It is easy to muster resistance against the blatant cruelty of collectivist dictators ... It is less easy to fight against the armies of those who are 'only here to help' – those who claim to come with the best intentions but come armed, all the same, with statutory powers and administrative instruments: education officers, children's officers ... welfare workers and other councils ... which claim to know best how to manage our private concerns. (1983, p. 173)

He particularly cites the example of communist states in seeking – like the Roman Catholic Church – to put allegiance to themselves as a higher priority than allegiance to another person. He critically examines the very limited and very inaccurate work of Marx and Engels on the family and their attempts to dismiss the 'bourgeois family'. In doing so he does not take into account that Marx and Engels were seeking to replace the 'bourgeois family' based upon ties to property with a freely chosen conjugal union rather than with some sort of communist promiscuity. Indeed Mount's vision of the blissful family is rather similar to that of Engels. His vision of the happy peasants and proletarians, relatively unregulated by the church, legal system and private property, as having the most free and unfettered marital relationships is actually very similar to what Engels too is saying. Unfortunately, this is also another myth. The working-class and agricultural families lived then as now in families which are just as patriarchal and unequal as many bourgeois families. For women, decisions to get married were more likely to have been based upon a need to escape an over-crowded domestic situation than on the attentions of a jolly local swain.

Mount examines the communist regime in the former Soviet Union as providing an example of state opposition to the family because the family threatens total adherence to communism. However, the Soviet Union is not a good example of this. In the Soviet Union some campaigners for free love – such as Alexandra Kollontai – were influential in the early post-revolutionary years, and at this time legislation was introduced to grant access to divorce and later on to abortion. It is unlikely that ideas of freely chosen conjugal relations were very influential outside of a small range of intellectuals, and they were quickly replaced in the early 1930s with a Stalinist puritanism. Except for these early years the monogamous, nuclear family was the officially sanctioned norm of the Communist state despite rising divorce rates. Furthermore, getting married was one of the main ways of gaining access to housing in the Soviet Union. Indeed, the family was viewed by the authorities as a way of controlling people: married folk were seen to be harder workers and more conservative in their activities. They could also be more easily threatened to enforce political compliance and families were held as 'hostage' for good behaviour or to ensure the return of travellers.

Other enemies of the family have included some extreme religious and political sects – from 'Ranters' to utopian communists – who in various ways have tried to replace the family with some sort of communal set of relationships. It is certainly the case that there have been some spectacular experiments in alternative styles of living over the centuries but these – as Mount points out – have been short-lived and precarious, certainly not sufficient to dent the dominant familial ideology. Another group of 'family-haters' cited by Mount are sociologists and psychologists whom he sees as a sort of secular priesthood. However, he really only uses the example of Lawrence Stone and Edward Shorter – both historians whose arguments for the historical relativity of childhood and love he refutes. He also cites the example of Sir Edmund Leach, who is in fact an anthropologist, and R.D. Laing, a psychiatrist. The sociologists he does refer to, such as Fletcher and Young and Wilmott, he cites approvingly. The family-haters he is attacking here were part of the 1960s critique of the bourgeois family, a trend which has long since been superseded by a more careful evaluation of family life and by new feminist and post-modernist critiques.

A further group of family-haters are the feminists, according to Mount. Here he criticises Germaine Greer, whose early feminist vision of sexual liberation as an alternative to monogamy was influential in the early days of feminism but is not one which is widely subscribed to now. Perhaps one of the reasons that he does not mention recent feminists is that their analysis of the family as being itself a totalitarian institution within which women's freedom is subordinated to men's does not fit very well with his libertarian philosophy.

Mount has a populist view of the family – he argues that his vision of the family is one practised by millions of 'ordinary' people throughout the centuries and by the working class and 'ordinary' families today. The historians had been biased by using only the examples of upper-class families which were not typical – whereas he used diaries and documents to reconstruct the lives of commoners who often resisted the state's or Feudal Lord's or church's attempt to regulate their lives. Hence, arranged marriages were not common amongst the classes with no property or status to protect.

This all indeed sounds much like the historical reconstruction of *socialist* historians. However, like Scruton he makes a connection between conjugal love, privacy and the accumulation of private property. Ordinary people, he argues, are driven to accumulate private property in order to provide for their children, and contemporary society simply provides them with more means to do so. Again, this connection is not proven. While he has ample examples of the existence of conjugal love, he has no examples of how this leads 'inevitably' to the accumulation of property. The link is not demonstrated, it is assumed.

Mount, however, claims that his view of the nuclear family is explicitly *not* patriarchal:

> I want to rely only on the evidence. And the evidence shows two things, as clearly as can be expected of any evidence concerned with times which are remote and with thoughts and feelings which are unlikely to be documented in the Public Records Office: first, as far back as we have any evidence at all, in Western Europe the ideals of love *and* equality were both present in the popular view of marriage; second, among ordinary people, to be happily married was always regarded as one of the most important pieces of good fortune in life. (p. 226)

Thus Mount is arguing that relations within the family were and are still equal and that in fact the family represents a set of maternal values. He criticises feminist historians (he does not say which) for presenting a picture of women in the past as downtrodden drudges, who served their husbands and were sexually neutered. As evidence of this, he uses examples of women's sexual demands on men, of women disobeying and leaving their husbands, of 'hen-pecked husbands' and of homes where women held more authority. He says we need to take account of women's resistance to patriarchal society. Many feminist historians would agree with him too. However, he cannot deny that these examples of resistance take place within the context of a patriarchal society where the odds were stacked against women: if they managed to own or control property themselves, this was in spite of the fact that the law on the whole did not allow this. If they were able to hen-peck their husbands and hold some sort of authority within the household, this is in the context of being disallowed from holding any office outside of the family. Mount's examples of emperors' wives and mothers having great influence only reinforces this: they held no influence outside of the family and family relations are structured by what goes on outside as well as what goes on inside.

Finally, Mount's example of women being business women by helping in their husbands' businesses and even running them while they were away is hardly evidence of equality within marriage. It is evidence of the fact that Mount is seeing the family in male terms. Women's role is secured by and located within the family in Mount's vision. His use of history to support this is selective. Whereas in some periods of history it was possible for women to own property or set up businesses this was always circumscribed, and in many other periods of history it was not possible for them to do this at all. Indeed women entered marriage because they had few alternatives: banned from public office, banned from education and not allowed to own or control property independently or earn a living, the Victorian woman could only become a spinster dependent on the family or a married woman dependent upon her husband. The legal rights of men and women within the family were certainly not equal, and if women were able to resist this they did so within an overall context of inequality. The fact that women resisted did not make them equal.

In his argument against feminists, Mount claims that he supports the fight for equal rights in public life and feels that feminists will soon have won that struggle. What is less acceptable is their attack upon the private sphere of the family. However, he claims that more extreme feminists will hold less and less influence as more equal public rights are won.

Mount's support for liberal feminism, along with his support for the right to cheap and easy divorce, aligns him with the liberal individualist strand within the New Right and against many of the more traditional conservatives such as Scruton and the Christian Right whom we described in Chapter 3. Mount's concept of equal rights in fact refers to a notion of formal equality which ignores the way in which women are hampered in the fight for recognition in public life precisely by their role within the family: they may now have equal opportunities to earn the same wage as men in the same jobs but, for women with family responsibilities in particular, they are not able to get to the same jobs. Furthermore, his idea of the family as a distinctly private sphere which should not be opened to state intervention and control is likewise a strand within New Right thinking. Like Roger Scruton he argues:

> ... among the first of these aspirations [of the urban working class] most intimate and ancient, is the desire for equality, privacy and independence *in marriage* ... it is difficult to resist the conclusion that

a way of living which is both so intense and so enduring must somehow come naturally to us, that it is part of being human. (pp. 255–6)

While he provides many examples of conjugal bliss, the darker side of the family is ignored. He is able to gloss over the fact that the state intervenes only with extreme reluctance when there is evidence of cruelty, neglect, sexual abuse and violence against family members. The 'privacy' of the family also shrouds many acts of terrible cruelty.

Furthermore, the fact that Mount takes a patriarchal view of the family conceals its convenience to men and oppression of women. Many of the examples he cites – for example, of relations between father and son or between husbands and wives – are ones where the woman is servicing the man and the rest of the family and where the man is in control and enjoying his sexual access and perpetuation of his name secured through the family. For example, he cites a quotation from Locke as an example of arguments for the 'natural' limits of patriarchal power:

The Father and Son are equally as free as much as Tutor and Pupil after Nonage; equally subjects of the same Law together, without any Dominion left in the Father over the Life, Liberty or Estate of his Son ... Nay, this power so little belongs to the Father by any peculiar right of Nature, but only as he is Guardian of his Children, that when he quits his care of them, he loses power over them ... (p. 181)

However, even if a man's natural right to control his sons may have ceased with the turn of the life-cycle, his control of the daughters continued to be absolute. What power could women exercise? We are not told because women exercising power was not even conceivable for Locke.

In another section Mount cites Erasmus approvingly as an example of:

stories of how forgiveness and mutual tolerance can repair marital rifts ... of the delights of both sexual and spiritual love. Sometimes, the dialogue sounds like the advice column in *Woman's Own*:

To Xanthippe, who wants to know how to make her husband kind and faithful, Eulalia replies:

'... See that everything at home is neat and clean and there's no trouble that will drive him out of doors. Show yourself affable to him, always mindful of the respect owed by a wife to a husband. Avoid gloominess and irritability. Don't be disgusting or wanton. Keep the house spick and span. You know your husband's taste; cook what he likes best. Be cordial and courteous to his favourite friends too. Invite them to dinner frequently, and see that everything is cheerful and gay there. Finally if he strums his guitar when he's a bit tipsy, accompany him with your singing. Thus you'll get your husband used to staying at home and you'll reduce expenses. At long last he'll think, "I'm a damned fool to waste my money and reputation away from home on a drab when I have at home a wife much nicer and fonder of me."' (p. 207)

This passage is cited approvingly as evidence of the universality of the nuclear family – that advice to the young wife in ancient Greece is really just the same as the homely and friendly advice on behaviour we can read in contemporary women's magazines. However, this is merely evidence of the fact that in Mount's vision of the family it is men who control. We might see this instead as evidence of a rather depressing continuity. Men hold office outside the family and the family provides them with sexual satisfaction and home comforts – even someone to sing for them when they are drunk. Women are there to provide these comforts and what the young wife herself would want in this extract is not considered. Her job is to make life so pleasant for her husband that he will not go off whoring, carousing and wasting money elsewhere.

In conclusion, we can see that Mount differs from Scruton in trying to show that the nuclear family is the product of free and unrestrained relationships which have resisted attempts by outside forces to control it. Like Scruton, however, he is arguing for the nuclear patriarchal family as being universal, natural and inevitable. In doing so he claims to use factual historical sources but in fact misuses both history and anthropology to create his case. He does this partly in order to show that the evil league of communists, feminists, welfare professionals, sociologists and psychologists is trying to undermine the family – a demonology which he shares with much of the New Right. To this he adds the church – which makes him different from the rest of the Moral Right. His view of both the family and the sources he is using is distorted by seeing them in male, patriarchal terms.

Finally, he views the family as somehow separate and different from the state, where in fact it would be better construed as a product of the state and increasingly sustained and reproduced by the state. The modern nuclear family, as we explain in the introduction, is to a great extent a product of social policies introduced since the nineteenth century (see also Wilson, 1977).

5

US New Right Intellectuals and the Family: George Gilder, Charles Murray, Martin Anderson and Lawrence Mead

In the US a number of writers have emerged, presenting intellectual arguments for the moral New Right. They were influential during Reagan's term of office and their work was read and referred to amongst Reagan's senior advisers and by the president himself. Here we have chosen to consider the work of four intellectuals: George Gilder, Charles Murray, Martin Anderson and Lawrence Mead. Some of their books have been best-sellers in the United States and have been re-printed more recently in Britain. It is likely that their ideas have had an important impact on popular consciousness and indeed they all write in a persuasive and popular style.

George Gilder

George Gilder is a journalist and writer who in the 1980s became program director for the International Center for Economic and Policy Studies in Manhattan. He has spent some time in London working at the Institute of Economic Affairs. He was one of the most influential intellectuals of the moral New Right in the US in the 1970s and early 1980s. His first book, *Sexual Suicide* (1973), a critical response to the feminist movement, was reprinted in 1988 as *Men and Marriage* after Gilder had become something of a celebrity. Gilder felt that the ideas were still relevant 15 years later. He argues that society is committing sexual suicide by following the path of sexual tolerance leading away from the traditional family. His arguments about moral degeneration are sociological rather than religious and he blames the sexologists, educationalists, left-wing liberationists, Black Panthers, gays and 'polymorphous perverts' for this new morality. To this list of degenerates he later adds assorted liberals, feminists and sociologists. These 'polymorphous perverts' are threatening to cheapen and demean sexual relations and – worse still – destabilise society by undermining patriarchal familial relations. In his book – written originally in response to the Equal Rights Amendment Campaign and the proposed 'Bill of Rights' for women which included provision for access to abortion, childcare and equal pay – Gilder argues that the 'sexual constitution of society' is being undermined:

> ... it is in these areas that the women most gravely impair the sexual constitution. It is here that they attack the male role, subvert poor families, incapacitate federal job and educational programs and generally prohibit any serious attempt to break the vicious cycles of poverty ... and engender a social crisis of unprecedented severity in American life. The 'progressive' programs of the feminists, in fact, simultaneously incite revolution and reaction, while undermining the most important source of stability in civilized society – the female role in the family. (1973, p.152)

How does he make the connection between such an unlikely variety of factors? He suggests that society needs the family as a basic stabilising force and that the family should consist of an economically and socially dominant male provider who will care for his dependent wife and children. This is a 'civilising' force: women tame men by managing them and thus creating good citizens:

> Female power, therefore, comes from what the woman can offer or withhold. She can grant to the man a sexual affirmation that he needs more than she does; she can offer him progeny otherwise permanently denied him; and she can give him a way of living happily and productively in a civilized society that is otherwise oppressive to male nature. In exchange modern man can give little beyond his external achievement and his reluctant faithfulness. It is on these terms of exchange that marriage – and male socialisation – are based. (1973, p. 23)

and

> Society has had to invest marriage with all the ceremonial sanctity of religion and law. This did not happen as a way to promote intimacy and companionship. It happened to ensure civilized society. (1973, pp. 73–4)

Without the family single men – whom he identifies as posing a major problem for society – will become a hazard to themselves and those around them by following their naturally aggressive instincts and predatory rhythms which are linked to sexual tension and release.

The key to singles failure is the profound biological dependence of men and women ... Men without women frequently become the 'single menace' and tend to live short and destructive lives – destructive both to themselves and society. (1974, p. 7)

Thus the importance of the family – and, in the family, women – lies in controlling men and integrating men into civilised society:

It is chiefly in the nuclear household that the man's connection to his children becomes indispensable. He is the key provider. His fatherhood is direct and unimpeachable and he identifies and provides for his offspring. His role as provider then becomes as crucial for the maintenance of the family as the mother's role. (1973, p. 88)

In this way, the family becomes particularly important in securing adherence to capitalism and in maximising economic productivity because a man with domestic responsibilities will work hard in order to provide for them (1973, p. 91).

Women, he argues, are naturally more monogamous and more altruistic. They have longer-term rhythms linked to the bearing and raising of children. It is their task to civilise men by subordinating them to female rhythms and preoccupations, turning them from feckless, purposeless 'naked nomads' of the bedroom into hardworking, tax-paying citizens with an orientation towards the future and a sense of responsibility. Hence, heterosexual monogamy and children give meaning to otherwise empty sexual encounters.

In his second book, *Naked Nomads: Unmarried Men in America* (1974), he goes into more detail to document the problems of single men. Bachelors (and lonely divorcees) are a hazard to themselves. They are four times more likely to commit suicide than other men, they are more likely to commit homicides, burglaries, rapes, to take drugs and to suffer from mental illness. They are more likely to gamble and be involved in crimes of violence and less likely to pay their bills, drive carefully or follow conservative politics. Consequently they are not only a nuisance to themselves but also a threat to the rest of society. Furthermore, an expensive law and order apparatus is needed to control them – an additional burden on the tax payer – and this too is an indirect consequence of feminism. This life, no matter in what glamorous terms it is portrayed, brings them little long-term satisfaction. Fighting, whoring and gambling are simply ways of demonstrating a masculinity which can be more securely affirmed only through responsible fatherhood and providing for a family. 'Because males cannot dominate the women in other ways, they resort to sex and violence' (1974, p. 114). However, paradoxically, powerful women can also render men impotent because masculinity is so fragile. Or they can drive men into masturbation, pornography or homosexuality.

The biological basis of Gilder's argument is apparent in these extracts. The reason for male behaviour is based on 'millions of years of evolution' and 'naturally' aggressive and promiscuous instincts. Gilder is arguing, however, that different forms of social organisation can tame these natural instincts in better or worse ways. The problem with contemporary society, as Gilder sees it, is that single men have not been satisfactorily integrated into acceptable social and economic roles. The permissive society and the feminists who have advocated sexual and economic equality have helped to produce a situation in which single women behave in the same sexually nomadic way as men (and thus make themselves unhappy by denying their real instincts) and where men feel put down by socially and economically successful women. If women are allowed to do this, there will be no incentive for men to become economic providers, because women can provide for themselves, and instead men will become demoralised, driven to crime and drugs to prove their masculinity in more destructive ways. If women are allowed equal wages and equal opportunities, he argues, they will achieve as well as, if not better than, men and will raise children without men's help. What incentive would they have to get married and turn their talents to civilising men? Clearly this must be stopped.

> A society of wealthy and independent women will be a society of eco-
> nomically predatory males, persuing the violent and short-term
> patterns of male activity learned on the battle field and in the hunt,
> or a society of narcoticised drones, who have abandoned sexuality
> altogether. The sexual power of women, if combined with economic
> power, leaves males with no civilised way to achieve sexual identity.
> If they cannot be providers, they have to resort to the muscle and the
> phallus. (1973, p. 97)

He further argues that granting women equality will create a crisis in the job market and 'selfish' middle-class women will take jobs away from less economically advantaged men who need them more. Thus, feminists cause male unemployment – especially amongst young men. These young men are consequently not seen as desirable marriage partners. Under these circumstances men will give up looking for work and attending jobs regularly. Consequently, he blames feminists for indirectly contributing to economic stagnation and family poverty. Even more pernicious, according to Gilder, is that the US welfare state pays for the independence of husbandless mothers by paying Aid for Families with Dependent Children (AFDC) and providing accommodation for them (benefits that would not be provided if they had an unemployed or low-paid husband). This can only perpetuate the problems of the ghetto by removing the male role as provider (poor males frequently cannot earn as much as women on welfare benefits) and encouraging women to deny and reject men.

> Welfare is one of the programs that not only does not work but also attacks our sexual constitution ... Our welfare programs – particularly Aid for Families with Dependent Children – is not a tragedy therefore because it gives inadequate aid. It is a tragedy because, as currently designed, it promotes social disintegration. (1973, pp. 133–4)

The long-term implication is that men will go around fathering children irresponsibly and women will choose to have children outside of marriage. Children growing up without a responsible male role model will perpetuate this pattern in a 'cycle of poverty'.

> In the welfare culture money becomes not something earned by men through hard work, but a right conferred on women by the state. Protest and complaint replace diligence and discipline as the sources of pay. Boys grow up seeking support from women, while they find manhood in the macho circles of the street and the bar or the irresponsible fathering of random progeny. (1981, p. 119)

The solution is to cut welfare (that is, non-contributory income maintenance) and to make single men therefore see the connection between sex and fatherhood, and for the US government to stop subsidising the economic independence of women. As an alternative, Gilder suggests the money should be spent on the men of the ghetto:

> Ghetto boys need preferential treatment; they need special training – special male affirmations – designed to overcome their relative disadvantages in relation to ghetto women. A job program that provides genuine equal opportunities for ghetto boys and girls will only reinforce the matriarchy. The girls, in general, will be better able to exploit the program and will thus increase their advantage. Social dissolution will be promoted. (1973, pp. 126–7)

Also, the claiming of benefits should be made as unattractive as possible to discourage dependency. This could be achieved by making eligibility more stringent and increasing the stigma which attaches to welfare claimants (Gilder, 1981).

Gilder points out that the poorest sections of US society and those most likely to be unemployed and existing on welfare are people in black neighbourhoods. According to Gilder, however, this is not on account of discrimination (which he thinks is largely something of the past) but because there are more single men and welfare mothers in black communities. Gilder tries to show that black women are far more advantaged relative to black men than are white women to white men; they even have higher IQs. The problems of black communities are exacerbated by anti-discrimination programmes which give black people access to positions without their having to fight for them and which removes their main incentive for self-improvement: poverty.

In a journalistic 'faction' biography, Gilder (1978) traces the life of a young black man called 'Sam' to illustrate how a matrifocal family and anti-discrimination programmes have served to disadvantage him. Sam is accused of raping a white girl, but Gilder illustrates how casual violence along with casual sex are a part of his everyday world. Denied custody or access to his child he sees himself as having no future and no prospects. So he fritters his life away in street-fighting which will one day destroy him. Hence his values are such that rape is just one way in which he can prove his brutalised masculinity.

In contrast to the unfortunate Sam, Gilder also wrote about the lives of entrepreneurs (Gilder, 1985) to show how the poor could overcome disadvantages of background and birth through determination and ingenuity. The book is designed to illustrate Gilder's theory of wealth and poverty which he had spelt out in his early writing: 'The only dependable route out of poverty is work, family and faith. After work the second principle of upward mobility is the maintenance of monogamous marriage and family' (1981, p. 74).

Spurred on by family responsibilities and a belief in themselves, the poor are able to beat the system through their own achievements. They are also able to overcome educational disadvantages but the education system, Gilder argues, institutionalises feminine values of conformity so that women and feminised men are better able to succeed. The increasing emphasis on credentialism, encouraged by equal opportunities legislation which requires recruitment on the basis of academic record, serves to further institutionalise feminine values. Men such as Sam feel demoralised when confronted with this, and it blocks their chances of social mobility. Not surprising then, Gilder argues, that there is a rising crime rate and a drugs problem.

In the early 1980s, Gilder fused his version of sociobiology with monetarist economic theory (Gilder, 1981). He argues that Britain – even more so than the US – has been economically handicapped by a 'bloated and arthritic' welfare state which has absorbed taxes while sapping morale and the entrepreneurial spirit. It is clear here that Gilder's version of economic liberalism requires an assumption of the patriarchal nuclear family. The family is good for capitalism and raises productivity: 'A married man ... is spurred by the chains of family to channel his otherwise disruptive male aggression into his performance as provider for wife and children' (Gilder, 1981, p. 75). And:

Husbands work 50 per cent harder than bachelors of comparable age, education and skills. The effect of marriage, then, is to raise the work effort of men by about half ... It is manifest that the maintenance of families is a key factor in reducing poverty ... The first priority of any serious progress against poverty is to strengthen the male role in poor families. (1981, p. 69)

By cutting back on welfare and encouraging enterprise and familial responsibility it should be possible to reduce the role of the state and provide tax cuts. Tax cuts would allow people's natural entrepreneurial spirit to emerge and men to become more responsible wage-earners. By 1981 Gilder, converted to economic liberalism, was arguing that welfare would be better replaced by private insurance schemes which encourage individuals to take responsibility for themselves and their dependents. From a theory about sex-roles this therefore became an economic theory and more obviously aligned with New Right politics. However, it has also taken on a further salience in the context of the rising unemployment and growing rate of crime and inner city disorders which have take place since he first published *Sexual Suicide*.

Furthermore, his incipient *laissez-faire* economic philosophy has progressed still further, since he now argues that anti-discrimination legislation is directly opposed to the interests of black people and of men generally and that the lower wages of women are determined by 'market forces' and should not therefore be tampered with. Indeed, he sees 'racism' 'sexism' and the 'myth of the exploited worker' as ideas invented by left-liberals, feminists and sociologists to justify the anti-discrimination and welfare programmes which give them so much influence and power. In his book on entrepreneurs (Gilder, 1984) he shows how people can overcome poverty, class and racial disadvantage through individual upward mobility. Sexism, of course, need not be overcome because it is necessary to society, so the entrepreneurs are all men.

The irony of Gilder's theory is that rather than arguing for the sub-ordination of women because of their biological inferiority, as do many of the moral New Right, he actually holds a very high opinion of women. He has no doubt that they can perform male social roles successfully as well as female ones. By contrast he has a very low opinion of men as being feckless, destructive and – without women's intervention – without purpose. He is indeed more extreme and outspoken in this view than are many militant feminists but, in a strange inversion of the feminist position, he argues that women therefore have to sacrifice themselves to men. He maintains that the focus should be on men by ensuring that they have useful roles as economic providers.

Like many of the other moral New Right intellectuals, some of his main arguments take issue with feminists and left-liberal intellectuals. However, much of his information actually comes from sociologists and feminists such as Jessie Bernard. As with other leading members of the moral New Right, he portrays feminists as seeking to eradicate sex differences, as denying biological destiny and as promulgating a creed of sexual license and promiscuity. Some of these points might perhaps resemble some aspects of liberal feminism, but on the whole this is a misrepresentation and gross over-simplification of feminist positions.

The arguments against promiscuity and the so-called 'permissive' society which lie at the heart of Gilder's early work are ones with which many contemporary feminists would in fact agree. The growing critique of pornography and sexual liberation developed by feminists through the 1970s has shown that this did not help to liberate women but introduced new layers of exploitation. Sheila Jeffreys (1990), for example, argues that it was simply a way in which male sexologists attempted to subordinate women to men's sexual needs and represented the apotheosis of phallocentric sexuality. Similarly, many radical feminists would instinctively agree with Gilder's early work in his analysis of the problems of society as lying with single men. However, his selective and cavalier use of statistics disguises the fact that racial and economic disadvantage overlay bachelorhood as indicators of social problems. Moreover, it ignores the problems caused by married men both within families and outside of them. Rape and violence are still masculine proclivities, but married men are better able to carry them out within the sanctity of their own home and thus cause less public nuisance. The lack of methodologically and sociologically informed interpretation of data undermines Gilder's work, reducing it to a series of braying assertions. However, more sophisticated analysis was provided by Charles Murray in the 1980s, whose work we consider later.

Gilder uses biological arguments to contend that men are instinctively and naturally aggressive because they are shaped by 'millions of years of evolution' as hunters. This viewpoint is based on myths of human evolution which are much vaunted but actually rest on little empirical evidence. In the animal kingdom we can find as many blueprints for a matriarchal society, for polyandry and for indulgent promiscuity as we can for a Darwinist monogamous patriarchy. While people are undoubtedly rooted in biological bodies, this lends itself to a range of interpretations and forms of organisation. During the 'millions of years of evolution' hunting did not necessarily form a very important part of human society and it is more probable that gathering food, animal husbandry and horticulture were more important, all of which were more often performed by women. (See

Linda Birke, 1980, for a critique of this kind of biological reductionism from a feminist perspective.)

The criticisms of the matrifocal, low-income black family echo other commentators (for example, Moynihan, 1965). It seems difficult for white men to conceive of a domestic arrangement at variance with a patriarchal nuclear family as being anything other than broken and deviant. Carol Stack (1974), however, has effectively demolished this idea by showing how the matrifocal family structure of low-income neighbourhoods in fact serves as a flexible and resourceful survival mechanism in a situation of extreme economic deprivation. Children can be cared for by female kin in a situation where men are likely to be unemployed and unable to support a family in any case and where women and men may need to be individually mobile in order to find jobs. Low-income black neighbourhoods are ones where black women have traditionally had to work in order to support families and where they have had to rely on informal childcare arrangements in order to do so.

Gilder's ideas and the way in which he assembles different kinds of information are designed to show that the poor are responsible for their own poverty and consequently serve as a justification for cutting welfare and introducing tax cuts for the rich. While collectivist and anti-discriminatory programmes have arguably failed to overcome poverty and discrimination, the sources of such failure are better sought in the racist and sexist ideologies which effectively neutralise attempts to overcome inequality through legislation (see Gregory, 1987). The rise in poverty is better accounted for by the overall economic recession of the 1980s in which inner-city and especially black communities were significantly disadvantaged and to which the sorts of welfare cuts which Gilder is recommending have greatly contributed. There is indeed not a shred of evidence to suggest that without income support black people would fight their way out of poverty: black men are unemployed because there are no jobs for them; black women are poor because they cannot find sufficient money from their own or from their partners' earnings to keep their families out of poverty, and cutting benefits would only make this worse. Because of the way in which Gilder argues his case and puts together causal chains of social trends, his work reinforces the popular sexism and racism which he claims no longer exists.

Charles Murray

Charles Murray has been described as the thinking man's George Gilder. He is an established social scientist who provides a more developed sociological perspective on many of Gilder's shriller journalistic generalisations. He also attempts to explore some of the philosophical issues behind his New Right recommendations for social policy which are grounded in many years of empirical research. He is presently working as a senior research fellow at the Manhattan Institute for Policy Research. His ideas were influential during Reagan's second term of office and his book on social policy, first published in 1984, was reputedly distributed amongst Reagan's cabinet and cited by Reagan himself in public announcements and speeches. His ideas are more influential than those of many far more established academic social policy analysts because he was able to enjoy promotion from the right-wing Manhattan Institute; they bore some of the initial cost of printing 20,000 copies of his book and sending some 700 free copies to leading politicians and journalists. Hence it was reviewed in all the leading newspapers and periodicals.

His ideas were developed through studies carried out in the 1960s of development programmes in Thai villages, from which he concluded that people in small communities are able to do more for themselves than intervention from above is able to do for them. The idea of the individual making rational choices and pursuing self-interest is also evident in this analysis – the individual of economic liberal thought (see Murray, 1977).

His work in the 1970s was concerned with juvenile justice, and here he produced some controversial conclusions which went against the grain of conventional left-liberal thinking. The conclusions of most studies had been that incarceration for juveniles is deleterious, turning them from ordinary delinquents – a stage which they are likely to grow out of – into hardened criminals who become recidivists. Consequently a range of non-custodial community alternatives had been developed to keep young people out of the criminal justice system. Murray and his associates, however, conclude the opposite. The best way of preventing crime, they argue, is by introducing harsh, swift and consistent sentences, with incarceration as the main punishment (Murray and Cox, 1979). Although this may not prevent recidivism, the authors conclude from their research amongst youths in Chicago that it has an important deterrent effect and hence punishment needs to be *seen* to be harsh in order to be effective. This idea is developed later in other ways. Murray's conception of what maintains good behaviour is fear of the penalties of acting wrongly.

The ideas gleaned from these empirical studies were developed more philosophically in *In Pursuit of Happiness and Good Government*, published in 1988. Again he develops his critique of left-liberal ideas of social policy by arguing that community, family and individuals are the only meaningful social units in a democracy and that these should be as far as possible self-governing rather than interfered with at a federal level. Like Reagan, he is against 'big government'. The role of government should instead be to enable people to pursue their own happiness and their own goals in their own way. This brings them pride and independence. The problem with state welfare handouts is that they destroy this sense of achievement; consequently, to remove the stigma from receiving benefits, they should be made repayable. Furthermore, like Martin Anderson, who we discuss later, he argues that if the welfare system did not provide for unfortunate individuals then private philanthropy would. Like Anderson too he sees private philanthropy decreasing as everyone comes to rely upon government.

By the late 1980s he also developed a theory of the 'underclass', a class which is defined by their behaviour and who need to be distinguished from the 'respectable' poor (Murray, 1990). His ideas about the underclass – already well known in the US – were publicised in Britain through a booklet published by the Centre for Policy Studies (this article also appeared in *The Sunday Times Magazine*). Here he argues that this underclass is growing in the US and that the 'disease is spreading', if more slowly, to Great Britain. He rejects the left-liberal view of poverty, which has purported that it is brought about by structural disadvantage. He argues that many so-called social problems are caused by people's behaviour and the sorts of choices they make, although he admits that these choices are conditioned by their environment – that is, by the community in which they live. According to him the three main indicators of the underclass are: illegitimacy, violent crime and dropping out of the labour force. Of these, he says, illegitimacy is the best indicator. While he sees all forms of single parenthood as being potentially harmful, unmarried mothers cause the worst problems because they are most likely to spend much of their lives being welfare-dependent. The increase in illegitimacy he sees as concentrated particularly in lower-class neighbourhoods. This is because for poorer women, he claims, living on welfare payments is less of a deterrent than for wealthier women. Unless they have financial deterrents or suffer from social stigma, young women will want to go around producing children because 'sex is fun and babies are endearing' and there will be nothing to prevent young women from enjoying both. As this happens so the community norms change. He thus sees the rise in illegitimacy as directly related to the increasing benefits available to single women with children and to the availability of council housing (or in the US public housing).

However, rather than seeing this as merely a changing trend he attributes many other social problems to it. The rise in crime he sees as paralelling the rise in illegitimacy, and not by coincidence. Male children growing up in female-headed households have no role models of responsible male figures and will therefore tend to run wild. If they live in neighbourhoods where other children run wild too, then this will become the established norm.

... in communities without fathers, the kids tend to run wild. The fewer the fathers, the greater the tendency. 'Run wild' can mean such simple things as young children having no set bedtime. It can mean them being left alone in the house at night while mummy goes out. It can mean an 18-month-old toddler being allowed to play in the street ... and it can mean children that are inordinately physical and aggressive in their relationships with other children. (*The Sunday Times Magazine*, 26 November 1989, p. 30, reprinted Murray, 1990)

Hence, children of single-parent mothers are more likely to drop out of the labour force, more likely to be involved in crime, more likely to take drugs, and so on.

Moreover, it also causes other problems. The males in these communities have no reason to strive to support families, no self-respect, and so they are likely to get into trouble – to develop a deviant lifestyle. An indicator of this is that they refuse to take up jobs. Murray uses the high drop-out rate on work experience programmes as evidence of this: '... the definitive proof that an underclass has arrived is that large numbers of young, healthy, low-income males choose not to take jobs (1989, p.35).' And:

... Just as work is more important than merely making a living, getting married and raising a family are more than a way to pass the time. Supporting a family is a central means for a man to prove to himself that he is a *mensch*. Men who do not support families find other ways to prove that they are men, which tends to take various destructive forms. As many have commented through the centuries, young males are essentially barbarians for whom marriage - meaning not just the wedding vows, but the act of taking responsibility for a wife and children – is an indispensable civilising force. Young men who don't work don't make good marriage material. Often they don't get married at all; when they do, they haven't the ability to fill their traditional role. In either case, too many of them remain barbarians (1989, p. 39).

The real problems for society are therefore the lower-class young males who are in this situation. Indeed, Murray sees a widening class gap with 'well brought up' and affluent young people working harder than ever but lower-class young people refusing to work at all. Although he explicitly denies that this has anything to do with being black – the trends are the same for all poor communities – he does say that Afro-Carribbean blacks in having a tradition of male unemployment and female-headed households are in advance of the trends.

What solutions does he envisage? One solution is the imposition of harsher sentencing:

> ... if the chances that one will get punished for a crime go down, then crime goes up. In every respect – the chances of getting caught, the chances of being found guilty and the chances of going to prison – crime has become dramatically safer in Britain throughout the postwar period, and most blatantly safer since 1960. (1989, p. 41)

A second solution is to stop handing out welfare to mothers with illegitimate children, thus deterring deviant life-styles. These ideas emerge directly from his earlier work but are applied now to the 'underclass' more generally and have developed a new stridency in the context of New Right thinking on moral issues.

In his influential book *Losing Ground: American Social Policy 1950–1980* (1984), he reviews changing levels of poverty and the 'Great Society' programmes of the Kennedy era in some detail. He argues that there is a 'poverty/spending paradox': that while poverty dropped, up until 1968, due to the general increase in affluence, it has risen since then at the same time as public expenditure has also increased. Moreover, Murray argues that unemployment rose despite a rise in Gross National Product over the same period, so that unemployment could not be the cause of the rise in poverty – government expenditure programmes were. He takes issue with the usual official definitions of poverty and wants to include 'latent poverty' in measurements of the numbers of poor – by this he means those who would have been poor if it were not for government support. However, he condemns this mainly on moral grounds:

> The reason for calling this the most damning of the statistics is that economic independence – standing on one's own abilities and accomplishments – is of paramount importance in determining the quality of family life. Hardly anyone ... would disagree. For this independence to have *decreased* would be an indictment of the American system whenever in our history it might have occurred. (Murray, 1984, p. 65)

This shows, he claims, that government spending programmes do not work and should be abolished. He also argues that the employment and poverty levels between black and white workers have diverged and that black workers are particularly likely to be unemployed and black women to be on 'welfare' despite increased government spending and growth in Gross National Product. This is partly, he argues, because the 'affirmative action' or anti-discrimination programmes of the 1970s, which gave black people jobs in order to break colour segmentation in the labour market, actually blocked mobility by giving them no genuine incentive to work hard and get educated.

He uses the example of an imaginary couple – Phyllis and Harold, with Phyllis as a pregnant woman. In 1960, he argues, Harold would have had an incentive to go to work and marry Phyllis. By the 1970s, however, the rules of the game have changed and as a result of the availability of various welfare benefits, they would be better off if Harold did not marry Phyllis and stayed out of work and Phyllis could then claim welfare for their illegitimate child.

Murray makes sociological as well as economic claims. He argues that the effects of welfare dependency have become part of the cultural expectations of the rising generation of poor (especially black poor) in a way that was not the case in the 1950s and before.

Murray attacks left-liberals in both Britain and the US for being soft on the undeserving poor and for blaming New Right social policies for poverty. Rather, he says that the policies recommended by left-liberals and put into practice in the 1960s and 1970s, policies such as community treatment for young offenders and support for single parents, have actually caused rather than solved the escalating problems of the 1980s. It is wrong to blame Thatcher or Reagan, he argues, because in fact Thatcher's policies have not gone nearly far enough. As such he takes on much of the conventional wisdom in Britain by using examples from the US.

There are problems in applying this analysis to the British context. The system of state welfare is more established in Britain and takes different forms. However, Murray's analysis of an underclass is to some extent accurate (even if the causes are not): poor people including single parents subsisting on benefits are driven into sink estates by the squeeze on jobs and housing, and the 'poverty trap' makes it difficult for people to come off benefits and take employment.

The problems of unemployment cannot be explained by 'work shy' adolescents. Studies carried out in the 1970s and 1980s have found consistently that young people (and adults) would have preferred to have jobs but that there were none available. Some would be worse off working due to the 'poverty trap' and many are sceptical of work-experience programmes which they recognise as simply ways to remove them from the unemployment queues (see Wallace, 1987). However, when jobs exist young people do work. Hence, the connections Murray makes here are the wrong ones. There is no evidence that children of single-parent families are more likely to be unemployed than those in two-parent families in the same neighbourhoods and circumstances.

Furthermore, the connection made between rising crime and rising illegitimacy is entirely spurious. There is no evidence that the children of single-parent mothers are more likely to be criminal than those of two-parent families in the same neighbourhoods and circumstances, although low-income neighbourhoods are more prone to crime. But low-income neighbourhoods have always been more prone to crime.

Finally, Murray's assertions about the child-rearing practices of single-parent families are based on no empirical evidence at all. It is just as likely that children of two-parent families are left to wander the streets unsupervised as those of one-parent families. Furthermore, Murray is able to produce no evidence that cohabiting relationships (which account to some extent for the numbers of children not born to formally married couples) are any less stable than married ones.

Other US scholars take issue with Murray's use of statistical material. They argue that poverty rose on account of rising unemployment (due to a weak recessionary economy) since the late 1960s. Also, as in Britain, the increasing numbers of elderly people have contributed to the rise in welfare spending programmes, hence the work disincentives – if they exist at all – are not as important as the economic and demographic factors causing poverty (Danziger and Gottschalk, 1985). Furthermore, both Danziger and Gottschalk (1985) and Greenstein (1985) argue that Murray's figures are inaccurate because the Great Society programmes have in fact served to decrease poverty and hardship; in fact the broadening of anti-poverty programmes lifted some 70 per cent of people, who would otherwise have been poor, out of poverty. The rise in Gross National Product which Murray cites did not necessarily lead to more jobs – in fact the number of jobs declined, leading to more poverty. Since 1965, Greenstein (1985) argues, programmes such as Medicaid, food stamps and nutritional assistance to mothers have led to a significant decline in infant mortality and improvement in the health of the elderly in poor areas. Furthermore, it is argued that Aid for Families with Dependent Children could not have caused the rise in illegitimacy because those who are claiming the benefit have suffered a significant drop in their living standards over this period – indeed the real value of AFDC has fallen by some 20 per cent since 1970 (Greenstein, 1985).

If Murray's thesis were correct, then, those states with the highest AFDC would also have the highest rate of illegitimacy – since the rate of payment varies widely from $120 per month in Mississippi to only $500 per year in California. But in fact this is not the case and there is no relationship between the level of AFDC and levels of illegitimacy (Bane and Jargowsky, 1988). Indeed, while the numbers of children in black female-headed households rose by 20 per cent between 1972 and 1980, the numbers claiming AFDC declined by 5 per cent. That is, those who raised children in this way did not necessarily claim AFDC. Indeed, in England, Ann Phoenix (1990) argues that the number of teenage mothers has declined in recent years rather than risen. Other research in the US, which Murray does not cite, showed little if any relationship between AFDC and out-of-wedlock births (see Ellwood and Bane, 1984). Furthermore, other academic research showed that the loss of jobs to black men was largely accounted for by the decline in the numbers employed in farming in the Southern states.

Finally, the example of Harold and Phyllis is misleading. Only in the state of Pennsylvania would this case have applied, and Pennsylvania was not typical in its payment of welfare benefits since welfare benefits grew twice as fast there as in the US as a whole. Murray also fails to take into account that Harold can claim food stamps if he is working in a low-paid job, so that there is less difference between the working and non-working income than Murray claims. Even in 1970, claims Greenstein (1985), almost anywhere in the country Harold would have been better off working than claiming welfare. In fact, no calculation is made of Harold and Phyllis's situation in 1980 despite the fact that the book is subtitled *American Social Policy 1950–1980*. This is because Harold would have been better off taking a low-paid job in nearly all states in 1980. Even in Pennsylvania Harold would have been a third better off working, because of the decline in the real value of AFDC over that period (Greenstein, 1985).

Hence there are ample reasons to doubt Murray's thesis on the basis of the assumptions he is making, and there have also been empirical refutations of his figures. Nevertheless, his book has been influential because it appeared to provide the ammunition which the Republicans wanted in order to attack welfare spending and the Great Society programmes, and it uses the ideology of economic individualism: blame the poor – especially female-headed households and black people – for poverty in the US. Thus Murray attempts to give racist and sexist ideologies an intellectual foundation; his arguments serve to justify popular prejudices. For this reason his arguments will be accepted by many people even if they are intellectually fallacious and his use of statistics highly selective.

Martin Anderson

Martin Anderson was economic and social policy adviser to Presidents Nixon and Reagan during their presidential campaigns and for periods whilst they were in office. In between he worked at the Hoover Institution, Stanford University, an influential New Right 'think tank'. In his own words Anderson (not a man who suffers from excessive modesty) described it as follows:

> ... With each passing year I become more convinced that it is the finest think tank in the world, unsurpassed in brilliance, distinction, and collegiality of my colleagues; unmatched in the richness of its research

resources; and located centrally on the campus of one of the finest universities in the world. (1988, p. xi–xii).

Anderson began his intellectual career with a study of urban renewal in the early 1960s when he argued – against what was then conventional wisdom – that urban renewal was disastrous for the poor and could not be achieved by federal intervention. Instead, he contended, it should be left to the 'invisible hand' of the private market to bring it about (1964, p. 228). Looking back on his achievements in *Revolution* (1988), he traces the rise and development of New Right thinking from the Barry Goldwater campaign in 1964 and makes very grand claims: 'The ultimate irony of the twentieth century may be that lasting, worldwide political revolution was accomplished not by Trotsky and the communists but instead by Reagan and the capitalists' (1988, p. 2). Indeed, looking around at the election of Margaret Thatcher in England, Brian Mulroney in Canada, Rajiv Ghandi in India and the developments towards capitalism in Eastern Europe and China, he concludes that the 1980s heralded: '... a time of profound revolution ... and an era of peace and capitalism' (1988, p. 3).

Revolution is a paean of praise to Ronald Reagan as a man, a politician and a statesman and includes a great many photographs of Martin Anderson himself. However, more important from our point of view is his volume *Welfare* (1978), which is the analysis of social policy which forms the basis of the social programmes he advocates. His views on social policy are that the War on Poverty initiated by the Democratic Party in the 1960s has now been won. 'There are many things wrong with our welfare system, but in terms of essentials, in terms of key goals it was set up to accomplish, it has been a smashing, total success' (1988, p. 3). Therefore, he concludes, it is time to dismantle the welfare apparatus which was set up to deal with poverty. The problem is that these programmes have developed a momentum of their own; they keep expanding, and the left-liberal establishment have a vested interest in keeping them in place by arguing that the poor are still there. More dangerous still, the left-liberal establishment are trying to introduce universal benefits which amount to a guaranteed minimum income for all:

> The institution of a guaranteed income will cause substantial reduction – perhaps as much as 50 per cent - in work effort of low income workers. As long feared by the public, and recently confirmed by independent research studies, such a massive withdrawal from the workforce would have the most profound and far-reaching social and economic consequences for society. (1978, p. 87)

In other words, if the left-liberal establishment had their way it would remove the will to work. Using a reinterpretation of official statistics, he argues that the left-liberal establishment have exaggerated the numbers in poverty: rather than the one in nine they claim, there are in fact less than one in thirty people in poverty. This is because they have not included non-income transfers in their figures – such as Medicaid and food stamps – which he argues increase the real income of poor families (although of course not everyone eligible may be claiming them and Medicaid does not feed, clothe or provide housing for a family). Indeed, he claims that because of all these benefits it is difficult for working families to be better off than those who are not working (although, as we have seen from Greenstein and other criticisms of Charles Murray, this is not actually true). He terms this the 'poverty wall', an inevitable consequence of welfare provision:

> The virtual elimination of poverty has had costly side effects. The proliferation of welfare programmes has created very high effective marginal tax rates for the poor. There is, in effect, a 'poverty wall' that destroys the financial incentive to work for millions of Americans. Free from basic wants, but heavily dependent on the state with little hope of breaking free, they are a new caste, the 'Dependent Americans'. (1978, p. 43)

Furthermore, he claims that the non-contributory income maintenance programmes known collectively as 'welfare' are not popular with the American people and should be reduced in favour of large tax cuts and an increase in defence spending. The remaining welfare should be targeted very specifically on the needy rather than being as generalised as it is at the moment .

The sort of comprehensive welfare programme recommended by the left-liberals would be politically disastrous and impossible to achieve without destroying the will to work, he claims. On these grounds he is very critical of President Carter's welfare programme (which was never implemented) and a range of other proposals to reform and simplify the complex array of poverty programmes and benefits. But what does he suggest as an alternative?

> Practical welfare reform demands that we build on what we have. It requires that we reaffirm our commitment to the philosophical approach of giving aid only to those who cannot help themselves while abandoning any thoughts of radical welfare reform plans that will guarantee incomes. The American people want welfare reform that ensures adequate help to those who need it, eliminates fraud,

minimises cost to the tax payers and requires people to support themselves if they can do so. (1978, p. 153).

More specifically, he argues that there should be a needs-only programme along with an attempt to eliminate fraud (which he sees as being substantial). This would remove rather than exacerbate the fear of stigma. There should also be a clear and consistent work requirement for receiving welfare: those who did not work should be removed from the register. Other welfare recipients who could also be removed include striking workers and students, neither of which are deserving categories in his view. Shirking fathers – that is, those that no longer live with their children but fail to pay maintenance – should be made to pay for their families. In his view there also should be an attempt to improve the efficiency of welfare administration – he claims that one-sixth of funds are frittered away on inefficient administration. Finally, responsibility for welfare should be shifted away from central government and towards the states and private institutions which are more in touch with public opinion.

Martin Anderson's ideas formed much of the basis for Reaganite social policies and provided a justification for rolling back the state and devolving it, for cutting welfare and for decreasing government spending. Anderson, like our previous two US New Right intellectuals, is arguing for a moral regeneration through cutting welfare programmes and, crucially for this, reasserting the role of the father as the provider and head of household. His ideas have other implications for the family too: by recommending a cut in welfare programmes, he really means cutting Aid for Families with Dependent Children, Medicaid, nutritional programmes for mothers and food stamps. Among the main beneficiaries of these programmes are single-parent families (usually headed by women) and poor women generally. Hence these cuts would particularly affect women and their families. However, they also affect women in other ways. Welfare programmes are among the main employers of women, and so this too would lead to a reduction in women's jobs.

Lawrence Mead

Mead's text on social policy – *Beyond Entitlement*, published in 1986 – is more moderate in its arguments but ultimately more extreme in its conclusions. Mead provides a philosophical justification for a point only touched upon by Anderson: the requirement to work for welfare.

My question is why federal programs since 1960 have coped so poorly with the various social problems that have come to afflict American society. These twenty-five years have seen a succession of new programs for the needy, disadvantaged, and unemployed pour forth from Washington. But during the same period welfare dependency and unemployment have grown, standards have fallen in the schools, and rising crime has made some areas of American cities almost uninhabitable. In all these respects there has been a sharp decline in the habits of competence and restraint that are essential to a humane society. The public never wished for this state of affairs, but government seemed powerless to affect it.

Part of the explanation, I propose, is that the federal programs that support the disadvantaged and unemployed have been permissive in character, not authoritative. That is, they have given benefits to their recipients but have set few requirements for how they ought to function in return. In particular, the programs have as yet no serious requirements that employable recipients work in return for support. There is good reason to think that recipients subject to such requirements would function better. (1986, p. 1)

Mead traces the history of welfare from the early 1900s through the 'New Deal' to the 'Great Society' era of reform of the 1960s and 1970s. The latter he sees as having five themes: the civil rights movement of the early 1960s which resulted in the ending of overt discrimination in voting, education and employment; the job-creation phase using Keynesian macro-economic policy; the introduction of special education and training programmes for minority groups in the mid 1960s; and then, most radical of all, the massive transfer of income to the poor through Social Security – that is, AFDC, Medicaid, food stamps and so on – which brought about what he sees as a staggering rise in welfare spending. More recently there have been attempts to overcome 'dual labour market' disadvantage by introducing 'affirmative action' programmes to recruit black workers into non-traditional sectors. The only one of these that he sees as being successful is the civil rights movement: the rest have failed monumentally.

The main problem, as he sees it, is that benefits were granted on a 'permissive' rather than an 'authoritative' basis – that is, they were *granted* rather than expecting something from the client in return. This creates dependency and an attitude that it is not necessary to give anything in return – a welfare culture. In one table he puts together the rise in numbers claiming AFDC, the rise in unemployment, the rise in serious crime, and the decline in educational aptitude scores to illustrate the fact that despite there having been massive government spending, indicators of social well-being have all declined while social problems have increased. However, he makes a more subtle argument for this than does Murray or Gilder.

He argues that the basis of citizenship should be work and a sense of obligation to the community. Welfare removes this. Therefore, all citizens claiming welfare should be obliged to work and should have their welfare removed if they do not. This, he maintains, is the basis of a free society (rather than representing a removal of civil rights and freedom as some critics have argued). It is liberating because it would avoid creating a dependent class of persons and this would help to erode the 'underclass' of unemployed dependents, many of whom are black. Like Anderson, he claims that economic growth and the income transfers of the 'Great Society' period have eliminated poverty apart from those (mainly black people) who have sunk into the underclass. This is a black problem because 47 per cent of black people claim welfare at some point. Like Murray he sees the underclass as the outcome of the rise in illegitimacy and irresponsible parenthood, particularly in black families. Moreover, members of the underclass are distinguishable from the 'deserving poor' because they have opted not to work and to support themselves. This non-work ethic has caused a fundamental change in the character of poverty, one which policy-makers and the left-liberals have ignored because they have ignored the *behavioural* bases of poverty – poverty, as he sees it, is caused by the behaviour of the underclass, and until that is changed it will persist:

> Non-work has caused a fundamental change in the character of poverty. Before 1960, and especially before 1940, poverty cut across the low-income population generally. Many working people could not earn enough to escape need,and those unable to work were even worse off. But after 1960 most of the aged and disabled were lifted out of poverty by expanded benefit programs, while a growing economy assured above-poverty incomes for the great majority of workers. The remaining poor were … mostly female-headed families and lower-class men, groups that usually worked irregularly or at best subsisted on AFDC or meagre local assistance programs.
>
> In recent years, whether families have working members, and how long they work, has been the main determinant of whether they are poor, next only to whether families are intact or single headed …
>
> The effects of more generous social benefits plus the family and work problems was to generate massive new dependency on government. Especially from the late 1960's on, millions of female-headed families and other low income groups signed up for AFDC, food stamps, and other programs rather than continue struggling to support themselves without assistance. (1986, pp. 37–8)

And:

Much of the remaining poverty in the US is due to high unemployment and non-work among the poor. If low-income men and welfare
mothers worked regularly, the underclass would be well on its way to
dissolution. (1986, p. 70)

From his research into the Work Incentives Program and 'workfare'
he argues that the underclass, mainly consisting of urban black
people, is characterised by women who can claim benefit without
working and men who can live in the black economy by welfare fraud
or by claiming benefit and who therefore have no incentive to work.
For some this amounts to a political protest against doing certain sorts
of menial jobs. This has led to a redefinition of normative standards
of behaviour in these communities. Mead argues, however, that in
so doing they are avoiding their duties as citizens. After all, he asks,
if the illegal immigrants can find work, why can the underclass not
do so?

He blames the fact that these issues have not been confronted on
the sociological thought which has coloured all political thinking since
the 1960s and is being promulgated by left-liberal reformers such as
Fox Piven, Cloward, Ohlin and Harrington. This cast of thought draws
attention away from the responsibility of the client and those at the
bottom of society and the problems of changing their behaviour and
instead blames the government and society more generally for not
doing enough to help the 'undeserving' poor. For example, the
behavioural issues raised in Moynihan's report in 1965 on the black
American 'problem family' were avoided because their problems
were put down to disadvantage or it was claimed that they were all
managing okay with an extended family structure. These reformers
have, Mead argues, also helped to create the idea that welfare is a right
amongst low-income communities by supporting organisations and
pressure groups campaigning for welfare rights. Hence, Mead contends
that when able-bodied young men refuse to work, this is a major
source of breakdown in the normative consensus that holds society
together.

So far, his assertions reinforce those of Gilder, Murray and Anderson
in arguing for the failure of welfare programmes and for the economic
individualist alternative – responsibility for oneself. However, there
are crucial differences between Mead and the other thinkers with
respect to women. Mead sees women – including mothers of young
children – as not exempt from the work ethic. He thinks that the
solution to welfare dependency is that they should go out to work
rather than get married and be supported by a man. He therefore
argues that welfare mothers too should be regarded as workers in the
1980s – since more and more women have joined the labour force,
family size has fallen and mothers seem to be able to find childcare
without government help when it suits them. George Gilder and

Charles Murray would see this proposal as leading to further moral decline if mothers were not present to prevent their children 'running wild' and if fathers were not present to provide role models for sons. These opposing views of women stem from a fundamental contradiction in New Right thinking. One the one hand, people are individuals with responsibility for *themselves*, but on the other hand women have a special status as being the responsibility of men, as do children. Hence, women are not individuals in quite the same way as men (see Abbott and Wallace, 1989). Thus, Murray and Gilder come down on one horn of this dilemma and Mead comes down on the other. Neither position is particularly helpful towards women, especially poor women.

Mead is critical of the existing workfare schemes and even of the introduction by Reagan of a work requirement for AFDC claimants. These measures do not go far enough. Nor is it sufficient to make work voluntary or to provide financial incentives to join work and training schemes. Work must be made an obligation for all claimants of welfare and the pool of potential workers widened – even some of the retired and disabled could be included. They would then pay taxes, and taxation is seen as a badge of citizenship: 'Only when work obligation seems as certain as "death and taxes" will non-work be overcome,' (1986, p. 143).

Consequently, he advocates the following measures:

1. Mothers should be defined as employable when their children reach the age of three (not six, as was the case when he wrote the book).
2. Mothers should be made to furnish their own childcare arrangements rather than depending upon government to do this for them.
3. The adjudication process should be shortened to make the obligations more effective and to avoid appeals (he mentions the role of welfare lawyers in obstructing workfare programmes).
4. Sanctions should be strengthened by removing benefits from the whole family, not just the non-compliant member.

Mead's influence can be seen from the ways in which his ideas informed the Family Support Act 1988 (see Chapter 6).

Mead outlines the moral duties of citizenship as follows – and here we can see he is aiming at ethnic communities particularly: to work; to support one's family; to learn to speak English; to learn enough at school to be employable; to abide by the law. The racism in Mead's thinking is also evident in these tenets of citizenship, since he seems to think failing at school and not learning English are examples of individual subversion of the American way of life.

Mead also differs from the other intellectuals mentioned here in that he argues that these measures should be imposed by central government, lest they be avoided by local states, whereas other US intellectuals on the whole recommend less of a role for central government and greater devolution to the local level.

Conclusion

It is evident that all the US intellectuals we have reviewed here share a common view that the welfare programmes of the 'Great Society' era are no longer useful and should be scrapped. Worse, they feel that they actually undermine the moral responsibility of individuals by removing their incentives to work and support themselves and by discouraging marriage. Their ideas of the family and the role of the family are particularly relevant in these arguments since they see welfare as having undermined the family – an institution crucial to the maintenance of social stability. A racist element is also evident in their thinking, and they hold strong opinions about men and the male role. The arguments about crime, welfare and the family in general have focused particularly upon the income maintenance benefits – especially Aid for Families with Dependent Children, since this (they claim) allows women to live independently of men and without having to go out to work. This is in fact a very small part of the Great Society programmes, but it resurfaced continually as the benefit which most offends them because it is seen as giving poor women too much autonomy. It offends them because it supports the poor and because it supports women outside of the family. Despite the fact that the connections between AFDC, illegitimacy and unemployment are completely unsubstantiated and rest upon assertions only, these anxieties about the male role and about welfare scroungers are ones which seem to touch a raw nerve in the American consciousness and hence provide intellectual support for the Republican enthusiasm for cutting welfare programmes more generally.

6

Putting Ideas into Practice (1): The Pro-Family Movement and Social Policy in the US under the Reagan Administration

Reagan's election as president in 1980 was seen as a victory by the New Right. In the United States the New Right, including the Christian New Right, had become politically organised in the 1970s and set out to give electoral support to right-wing candidates. While it did not exclude the possibility of supporting other candidates, in practice the movement worked throughout most of the 1980s for the election and re-election of right-wing Republicans. Earlier aspirations to be a 'third force' in politics or to form a third party were all but abandoned, and major efforts were directed towards being a strong force within the Republican party and mobilising potential voters (often by registration campaigns) to vote Republican in national and local elections. However, political pressure group activities were wider than this. As was pointed out in Chapter 2, the New Right in the US in the late 1970s set out to co-ordinate a large number of single-issue groups and continued to do so at a local as well as a national level throughout the 1980s – particularly those groups agitating for reforms on 'moral issues' such as school prayers, abortion, and the teaching of Christianity in schools.

In the late 1970s the Right Wing in the US discovered a candidate who seemed to be able to fulfil their aspirations. Ronald Reagan had been governor of California between 1966 and 1974, and during this period he had instituted a programme of radical-right reforms. When he stood for presidency he developed these ideas further into what later became known as 'Reagonomics'. They included: large across-the-board tax cuts; government control of the rate of growth of the money supply to control inflation; a large reduction in public spending, especially welfare benefits; a large increase in defence spending; extensive de-regulation of the economy; an opposition to 'Big Government' (i.e. extensive intervention by government at the Federal level); and a desire to return more control to the individual states (King, 1987). These economic changes were complemented by Reagan's passionate moral defence of freedom – which meant freedom from paying taxes and freedom from government intervention – and

98

a condemnation of communism. A link was made between capitalism and Christianity so that God was thought to support free American imperialism and communism was thought to be the work of the devil and the forces of evil – an idea also propounded by television evangelists. Thus the struggles for political freedom in Latin America could be seen as the work of evil communist infiltrators and brutally crushed by US intervention in the confident belief that such intervention was backed by God.

Both in his presidential election campaigns and while in office, Ronald Reagan gave strong vocal support to the New Right and the moral programme of the Christian New Right. In the 1978 presidential campaign he endorsed the Christian New Right (Jorstad, 1987). He supported issues such as constitutional amendments to restrict the right to abortion and to permit school prayers. He put himself firmly on the side of the 'pro-family' movement in supporting both the patriarchal nuclear family as necessary and inevitable and in seeing welfare reforms as at least partly responsible for the decline of the American family. He agreed that there should be strong government legislation to sustain a 'moral order' while also supporting the view that Big Government should reduce its intervention in the economy and the 'private' sphere of family life. In his 1980 acceptance speech Ronald Reagan declared:

Let us make them a new beginning ... let us make a commitment to teach our children the values and the virtues handed down to us by our families, to have the courage to defend these values and the willingness to sacrifice for them.

Let us pledge to restore in our time the American spirit of voluntary service, of co-operation, of private community initiatives. A spirit that flows like a deep and mighty river through the history of our nation. Work and family are at the center of our lives, the foundations of our dignity as a free people. When we deprive people of what they have earned ... we destroy their dignity and undermine their families. We cannot support our families unless there are jobs and we cannot have jobs unless people have both the money to invest and the faith to invest it.

In his acceptance speech at the Republican Party Convention he had made even clearer his support for the 'moral' agenda of the Christian New Right.

We reaffirm our belief in the traditional role and values of the family in our society ... We affirm our support of a constitutional amendment to restore protection of the right to life for unborn children ... We protest the Supreme Court's intrusion into the family structure through the denial of the parents' obligations and rights to guide their minor children. (quoted Eisenstein, 1984, p. 27)

Ronald Reagan explicitly supported the New Right 'pro-family' ideology of the sanctity of motherhood and the traditional patriarchal nuclear family. He agreed with their view that in order to maintain the economic and political strength of the United States it was necessary to strengthen the family as the basic building block of society. He agreed with the free-market liberals that it was not only (or necessarily mainly) changes in morality that were undermining the family, but the growth of the welfare state and specifically of Social Security benefits that enabled women and their children to live independently of husbands and fathers. In a radio broadcast in December 1983, Ronald Reagan stated that: 'There is no question that many well-intentioned Great Society-type programs contributed to family breakups, welfare dependency and a large increase in births out of wedlock' (Quoted in Moynihan, 1986, p. 69).

These same welfare benefits of course enable husbands/fathers to avoid their responsibilities to their (biological) families and fail to motivate them to remove themselves from poverty. This argument was clearly expressed by Paul Craig Roberts, First Assistant Secretary to the Treasury for Tax Policy in the Reagan administration when he testified in January 1985 before the Senate Finance Committee:

> The growth of government has brought on enormous transformations in the nature of US society. Over most of our country's history, there was neither an income tax nor a welfare system.
>
> This was a period during which the economy simultaneously absorbed millions of penniless immigrants, many of whom could not even speak the language, and rapidly reduced the poverty rate. *Today poverty has been institutionalised by the government's poverty programs, and the poverty rate no longer declines.* In the US today, the illegal poor – aliens who do not qualify for the government transfers and welfare programs – are consistently able to work themselves out of poverty. By undermining private property, a welfare state restricts opportunities for all on the grounds that otherwise some will succeed more than others. (quoted in Moynihan, 1986, p. 70, emphasis in the original)

As with the Thatcher administration in Britain, the Reagan administration in the US expressed both a commitment to 'pro-family' issues and to reducing the role of the welfare state and explicitly argued for a connection between the two. Thus the defence and restoration of the traditional patriarchal nuclear family combined an emphasis on 'moral' and economic issues – the rejection of the Equal Rights Amendment, hostility towards abortion, the retention of school prayers as well as tax cuts and the dismantling of the welfare state were all seen as measures that would stabilise the patriarchal nuclear family. The Reagan administration supported both unfettered free-market capitalism and moral authoritarianism – and indeed supported the Christian New Right view that the latter was essential to the former.

In evaluating the extent to which Reagan's administration actually carried through measures that were in accordance with the programme of the New Right and its own expressed commitment to them it is necessary, as Gillian Peele (1984) has pointed out, to recognise important differences between the United States's and the British political systems. In Britain, the prime minister can generally command a majority in the legislature (Parliament) for measures put forward by the government. There is strong central government control in Britain, with little local autonomy, and indeed the power of local government has been reduced in Britain under Thatcher administrations. The power of the courts is also very limited – restricted to the interpretation of legislation on appeal. Thus, once elected, a British administration has virtually unfettered power to enact its programme of reforms. The situation is very different in the United States. The separation between the executive and the legislative (the Senate and Congress) places limitations on the power of the president. A president may or may not have a majority of his party in one or both of the houses, and even if he does party loyalty is not as strong as in Britain, where it is extremely rare for members of Parliament not to vote with their party. Thus the legislature can delay or even veto measures put forward by the president. The states in the US also have considerable autonomy, both in passing legislation of their own and in the implementation of federal legislation. For example, Aid to Families with Dependent Children – the main welfare (non-contributory means-tested benefit) in the US – is a federal measure, but the amount paid to recipients varies considerably from state to state. The Supreme Court also has power in the area of legislation, especially in the interpretation of the constitution. Presidents can influence the Federal Judiciary not only during their terms of office but long after they have left office by their power to nominate Supreme Court judges. Reagan sought out candidates who opposed abortion and affirmative action and who supported capital punishment and states' rights. Thus the legalisation of abortion in the US comes as a result of a Supreme Court decision – Rex vs Wade in 1973 – based on an interpretation of the right of women under the constitution. A constitutional amendment must be approved not only by both federal legislative Houses but must also be ratified by three-quarters of the state legislatures. Thus the Equal Rights Amendment (ERA), aimed at giving women equal rights under the constitution, was passed by the House of Representatives and Senate in 1973 but failed to be ratified in the required number of states.

Moral Policies

While the New Right saw the election of Reagan to the presidency as a victory for their position, they continued to lobby central government and to target local government – for example, on the Equal Rights Amendment (ERA) and over the control of school textbooks. Victories for the New Right at the local level may have little or nothing to do with the federal administration; for example, the ERA was virtually defeated while Carter, who supported it, was still president. On the other hand, the lack of enactment of New Right policies may result not from a lack of commitment by the president and his administration but from opposition by a majority in Congress or in the local state legislatures.

Although it is impossible to separate fully the 'moral' and the 'economic' agendas of the New Right, we will look at these two sets of issues separately. Examining the extent to which the support of the Reagan administration for the 'moral' and 'economic' policy proposals of the New Right has been enacted more generally, we will be concerned to consider how families and family life have fared under the Reagan administration.

In terms of 'moral' issues, a number have been central to Christian New Right policy proposals, often arising out of reaction to specific rulings of the Supreme Court – rulings that have, for example, legalised abortion, restricted religious exercise in public schools and decreed that creationism (the biblical account of God's creation of man and woman, renamed 'creation science' by the Christian New Right) does *not* have to be taught alongside Darwinism in biology lessons. The New Right have also been committed to preventing the ratification of the Equal Rights Amendment, to restricting pornography and to limiting the legal guarantee of civil rights for homosexual men and lesbian women. These issues taken together are seen to be pro-family – to be concerned with strengthening the traditional nuclear family, the biologically, God-given role of men and women within that family and the rights of parents to control the 'moral' education of their children. Many of the key policy objectives of the Christian New Right were included in the Family Protection Bill sponsored in the Senate by Roger W. Jepson (Republican, Iowa) and Paul Laxalt (Republican, Nevada) and in the House of Representatives by Albert Lee Smith (Republican, Alabama). The bill in its preamble stated that it intended: 'to strengthen the American family; to protect [its] integrity, to foster and protect [its] viability by emphasising family responsibilities in education, tax assistance, religion and other areas related to the family and to promote the virtues of the family' (quoted by Jorstad, 1987, p. 81).

If passed, the measures would have enacted '[an] important Christian New Right proposal for combating the secular humanists on matters of public morality and family issues' (Jorstad, 1987, p. 81). These included: the notification of parents if contraception or abortion services were given to unmarried minors by federally-funded agencies; the forbidding of the use of federal funds for educational material that 'denigrates the role of women as it has been historically understood'; the permitting of school prayers; parental rights in overseeing a child's education, including religious education; local state autonomy in legislating in areas of juvenile delinquency, child abuse and spouse abuse; and the exemption of religious organisations from affirmative action quotas (Jorstad, 1987, pp. 80–1).

The key clauses of the bill redefined the family and were designed to ensure that parents could exercise responsibility for their children – especially for their moral and religious education. Although the Bill was debated during 1981 in both houses, it was never voted on. However, the Reagan administration did demonstrate its support for a number of measures in the proposed legislation, and in July 1982 it opened 'Family Forum 11' wherein the government expressed its support for the family policies of the Christian New Right, which in turn actively campaigned for government proposals to be brought forward in this area.

An important issue for the Christian New Right, often portrayed as an educational matter rather than a familial one, was the question of the role of religion in public (state-provided) schools. However, the issue goes to the centre of concerns about the family and particularly the patriarchal nuclear family. It focusses on the right of parents both to control the moral and religious education of their children and to ensure that they are taught 'pro-family' (anti-feminist) and 'pro-moral' (anti-gay) values.

These issues often come to be seen as part of the fight against 'secular humanism'. This concept is never well defined but is generally understood to be the view that people control their own destiny. It is therefore claimed by the New Right to be religious, thus making it unconstitutional for it to be taught in schools. Three specific issues are central: school prayers, school textbooks and the teaching of creationism. The activities by the Christian New Right on behalf of these issues predate the election of Ronald Reagan, but it was thought that real action might at last be forthcoming under a president who gave vocal support to them. In May 1982 Reagan presented to the Senate a proposal that 'Nothing in this Constitution should be construed to prohibit individual or group prayer in public schools or other public institutions. No person shall be required by the United States or any state to participate in prayer.' However, opposition to the measure was strong, and despite an amendment by Senator Jesse Helms (Republican, North Carolina) preventing the Supreme Court from ruling on school prayers (on which Reagan said he would take no position), the measure failed to receive the necessary two-thirds majority. In 1983 the administration introduced the School Prayer Amendment, reworded to read: 'Nothing in this constitution shall be construed to prohibit individual or group prayer in public schools or other institutions. Neither the United States nor any state shall compose the words of prayers to be said in public schools.' Again, the proposal failed to gain the necessary support. However, an act was passed in 1984 giving students in secondary schools who wanted to explore religious views 'equal access' with other students to use school premises for extra-curricular activities. Non-school personnel were, however, explicitly excluded from participating in such student meetings; attendance was to be voluntary and not recorded.

While federal law makers had not passed a constitutional amendment permitting school prayers, a number of states had (by 1984) enacted measures permitting a 'moment of silence' at the beginning of the school day. In 1984 the House of Representatives passed a measure requiring schools to allow silent prayer in classrooms, but the Senate failed to take up the matter. In 1985 the Supreme Court ruled that when 'moment of silence' legislation had a religious purpose it was unconstitutional. Nevertheless, in 1985 the Oval Office confirmed that the administration still supported a school prayer amendment. By this time no headway had been made on the New Christian Right agenda of legislating for school prayer, nor had they been able to get the teaching of creationism given equal time with Darwinism in the biology syllabus, nor had they obtained greater parental control over textbooks or syllabuses or public schools more generally. However, a measure was passed in 1984, The Protection of Pupils' Rights Act (Hatch Amendment), which was fully supported by President Reagan. The new regulations required that parents give their consent before students could be asked to provide information about their political affiliations, mental or psychological problems, to appraise their family critically or to reveal their family income. The Christian New Right attempted to mobilise parents to use these regulations to monitor what was taught in the classrooms. The new secretary at the Department of Education, William Bennett, encouraged this: 'I would take a very close look at what my son was being asked to study, because there are lots of things in schools ... that don't belong there' (*Congressional Record*, 1985, p. 17). However, it became evident that the Hatch Amendment did *not* apply to all curriculum material, but only to federally-funded programmes of research. The Christian New Right then attempted to get legislation passed at state level giving parents control over the curriculum, but they were not successful.

A fight clearly allied to this has been 'the school textbook protest movement' aimed at removing books that contain secular humanist ideas from school libraries and classrooms and prohibiting as school textbooks those that teach secular humanism. This movement has had some successes, especially in Texas, where one committee chooses all the state's public school textbooks.

Related issues are the state funding, tax exempt status and state accreditation of religious private schools. Discontent with the state schooling system led Christian New Right parents in the 1970s to form their own Protestant Christian schools where their moral values could be central to the curriculum. However, these schools were expensive to found and run and relied on parental payment of fees. Two issues arose, on both of which the Christian New Right received strong support from President Reagan: financial support to parents who did pay school fees, and tax-exempt status for New Right Christian Day Schools. When he came to office Reagan gave support to the idea of a tax-voucher system which would give tax relief to parents who paid fees for their children's schooling. A tuition tax-credit proposal was introduced in the Senate in 1981, with the president's support. In 1983, when it seemed likely that this measure would not get through, the Reagan administration proposed a revised plan which would provide tax-relief only to parents on low or middle incomes on a sliding scale. However, this measure fell because it was not voted on before the 1984 election. The Reagan administration also failed in its attempt to enable schools which practised racial discrimination (as at least some Christian New Right ones do) to enjoy tax-exempt status, removed as a result of the 1978 IRS (Inland Revenue Service) decision to enforce regulations against such schools.

One battle in which the Christian New Right did have some success was over state accreditation of their schools – although here the federal government was not involved. A number of states attempted to close down Christian New Right schools that did not have state accreditation. The Christian New Right claimed that requirement of state accreditation violated constitutional rights of free exercise of religious and parental control. Although the Christian New Right lost in court in Nebraska they won in Maine – and even in Nebraska the state officials had to compromise in the end and allow the schools to remain open.

In terms of parental control over education, despite the strong support of the Reagan administration the New Right have not been notably successful, although they have won local victories and kept the issue on the public agenda. Neither have they been significantly more successful in achieving legislative changes in other areas of social or family concerns.

Abortion has been one of the primary issues, with the Christian New Right – supported by other groups – attempting to get abortion banned or restricted. The Roe vs Wade decision in 1973 did not give women the right to decide on abortion, as is often argued, but rather gave the power to medical practitioners. Nevertheless, it was a victory for women. However, even before President Reagan, who openly voiced his opposition to abortion, was elected to the presidency, women's right had been eroded. The rights of poor women to an abortion were virtually brought to an end in 1977 and 1979 when Medicaid funding was removed (money being available only if the woman's life was endangered). However, despite Reagan's commitment to the anti-abortion cause, no legislation was passed during his term of office that further restricted women's access to abortion. Indeed, anti-abortion groups blamed the Reagan administration for the failure of an amendment to a bill on the national debt ceiling which, by making a declaratory non-binding statement about total 'personhood', would have imposed a permanent ban on federal funding of abortion services and encouraged the Supreme Court to rescind its decision in Roe vs Wade. It was suggested that the administration had not supported the measure sufficiently strongly. However, the Department of Health and Human Services has issued regulations requiring the complete segregation of abortion facilities and other family planning services in federally-funded clinics and hospitals. According to Christine Peele, this is intended:

> to circumvent the legislative process and wield the threat of denial of funding so that clinics and hospitals will suspend abortion services. In this way, the New Right and the state may intend less to recriminalise abortion than to de-legitimise it by rendering it inaccessible and marginal once again. (Peele, 1984, p. 269)

The New Right concern with reproductive rights extends beyond abortion; they argue that sex is only legitimate within heterosexual marriage. They have opposed contraceptive advice and abortion for non-married women and demanded that both parents give their consent or be informed if their minor daughter seeks advice about contraception or abortion. Reagan appointed administrators to the Department of Health and Human Services who were not only anti-abortion but also opposed to the recognition of teenage sexuality. This was reflected in the enactment of federal regulations under Title X of the Public Health Services Act, requiring federally-funded family planning projects to notify *both* parents or the legal guardians within ten days of giving birth control devices or pills to any minor (Peele, 1984, p. 269). The courts have, with qualification, tended to endorse state requirements for parental consent to or notification of teenage abortions.

The Christian New Right are also opposed to homosexuality because it challenges their view of what it means to be a 'man' and to be 'masculine'. For the Christian New Right, to be masculine is to be married and to be the dominant figure within the heterosexual nuclear family. As a result of Reagan's cutbacks in the social welfare budget, federal legal services to homosexuals have been curtailed. The New Right have also had some success in defeating gay rights ordinances in some cities, denying federally-funded legal services to homosexuals and banning homosexuals from teaching in public schools.

The New Right are also anti-feminist – that is, they are against women having the same rights as men. They argue that women should fulfil their traditional role in the family caring for their husbands and children. They wish to revalue the role of the housewife. A major victory for the New Right was the defeat of the ERA (Equal Rights Amendment). However, although Reagan made clear his opposition to the amendment's ratification, it was evident before Reagan was elected president that it was unlikely to receive the necessary support.

While Reagan gave considerable support to the New Right – and appeared to share their moral values during his terms of office – their moral agenda has not been implemented. The Christian New Right has been a strong pressure group, advocating legislation on a wide range of 'moral' (social) issues. It has claimed strong electoral support and has certainly organised itself as a powerful political lobby, using television and radio as well as more traditional means to weld together a number of single-issue groups. However, it is probably not as strong as it likes to portray itself as being or as a number of commentators have suggested that it is (Bruce, 1990). It seems unlikely that its moral agenda has majority support in the United States, and there is no evidence for a shift to the right in the United States on 'moral' issues in the 1980s; if anything, there has been a shift to a more liberal position (Bruce, 1990, p. 166). While Reagan continued his commitment to the Christian New Right throughout his presidency and George Bush made a similar commitment in his 1988 election campaign, the political focus has, in fact, been on the domestic economy and on foreign policy issues. Thus, while the moral and Christian New Right argue it is necessary to resolve moral problems because morals provide the necessary basis for a strong capitalist society, in practice Reagan concentrated on the economy.

Economic Policies

In the United States in the 1980s, as in Britain, economic policies had an effect on families. Some aspects of economic policies explicitly reflected the influence of New Right criticisms of welfare – the view that welfare has enabled the establishment of deviant family forms, especially single-parent families headed by women. While not all domestic economic policies are explicitly directed at families, they can have unintended consequences as well as intended ones. Arguably, taxation policies fall into this category. However, the combined effect of Social Security and taxation policy in the US under Reagan was to advantage the better off and to disadvantage the poor, whether they live in traditional families or not. Ethnic minorities and women whose independence and economic security were most under attack by the economic policies of the Reagan administration were particularly hard hit.

Reagan was elected to the presidency, as Mrs Thatcher was elected prime minister, on the promise of reducing taxation. Like Thatcher, Reagan argued that reducing personal and corporate taxation would provide incentives at both ends of the income distribution. On coming to office in 1981, Reagan introduced a budget that both cut income tax and reduced expenditure on welfare programmes. As in Britain, the main effect of the tax cuts was to advantage the higher wage-earning families while the major attack on welfare was on means-tested (non-contributory) benefits. Taken together with the recession of the late 1970s and early 1980s, which resulted in high levels of unemployment and economic restructuring, the effects have been similar to those in Britain. There was a reduction in real wages in private industry in the 1980s – real wages were lower in 1987 than in 1980 (*Statistical Abstract of the United States*, 1989, Table 661, p. 404). Economic recession and high levels of unemployment have made lower real wages acceptable to trade unions. Unemployment often leads to a return to the labour market at a lower level of income. Job growth in the 1980s was concentrated in relatively low-paid jobs (Harrison and Bluestone, 1988). While average household income increased slightly (6 per cent) between 1980 and 1987, this is because of an increase in dual-earner households (*Statistical Abstract* 1989, Table 712, p. 440). These economic changes have thus disadvantaged traditional single-earner households and put pressure on families to have two earners – indeed, to the extent that it is now suggested that it is normal for both partners to have paid employment even when they have young children.

These changes also resulted in a widening of differences in income between the better-off and poorest families in the United States during the 1980s. Between 1980 and 1987 the bottom fifth of families' share of income declined by 0.6 per cent while the highest fifth increased its share by 2.1 per cent (*Statistical Abstract*, 1989, Table 722, p. 446). Black families fared even worse. While black family income was 60 per cent of white family income in 1980, by 1987 it had declined to 56 per cent (*Statistical Abstracts*, 1989, Table 721, p. 445). The proportion of the population in poverty also increased. Using the official poverty line, adjusted for household size, the proportion of households in poverty increased marginally, from 13 per cent in 1980 to 13.5 per cent in 1987 – eight million were added to the numbers of officially poor, three million of them children (*Census Bureau*, 1988, p. v). However, using the more realistic measure of poverty as the poverty line plus 25 per cent, the increase between 1979 and 1987 was 3.7 per cent. (The official poverty line in the US is a very basic minimum – in 1984 it was $10,609 for a family of four. In the same year, a Gallup poll found that the median amount the public thought a family of four [two parents, two children] could get by on was $16,000 – Gallup, 1986.)

There has been an increase in the number of children living below the official US poverty line – for example, over 50 per cent of all African-American children now live in households below the poverty line (Miller, 1990). The rise in child poverty between 1979 and 1985 was greatest for Hispanic children (an increase of 43 per cent) followed by white children (37 per cent) and the least for black children (6 per cent – see Sandejur, 1988, p. 50). During the late 1980s about a third of all Americans depended to a greater or lesser extent on welfare benefits.

The chances of moving out of poverty also decreased in the 1980s. Although this has been blamed on the rising number of single-parent (mother-headed) families, the Michigan Panel study of Income Dynamics suggests that other demographic shifts should have increased chances of escaping poverty. Thus while single-parent mothers have a lower chance of exit, fewer families were large or were headed by someone without high school education (Adams *et al.*, 1988). The key factor is that income inequality has increased – the depth of poverty of some being so great that they cannot escape. In 1987 about two in five poor people had incomes of less than half the official US poverty line (US Congress, 1988, p. 12). Also, the main decline in income has been among the young. ' Virtually the entire burden of rising income inequality of the 1980s ... has fallen upon younger people, especially the under 35s.' So it was that the median income of American families with children headed by someone under 25 dropped by an astonishing 63 percent from 1979 to 1986 (Cornel, 1990, pp. 303–4). The conditions under which the poor lived in the United States in the late 1980s are illustrated by health statistics: between 1980 and 1985, more US children died of poverty, hunger and malnutrition than the total number of US battle deaths in the Vietnam war. (On average, one child died every 50 minutes.) The chances of a poor white or black child dying during the first year of life were twice that of a child from a higher-income family. Thirty-six per cent of US children had no health insurance coverage. Under Reagan the infant mortality rate increased, reversing a trend of decline. The gap between the infant mortality rate of the low-income and high-income families also increased. The number of families who were refused medical care because they could not afford to pay increased by two million between 1982 and 1985 (National Rainbow Coalition Health Commission, 1988).

In terms of budget cuts in social programmes, the main cuts under Reagan were in welfare programmes. As in Britain, the tax transfers that benefit the better off (mainly tax relief on mortgage interest payments) have not been reduced, nor has there been the same level of cuts in Social Security benefits that are based on contributions – for example, Medicare, unemployment pay and Old Age Pensions. Under Reagan, tax exemptions were the fastest growing form of hidden welfare, increasing from $93 billion in 1975 to $355 billion in 1985. Some benefits do accrue to low-income people because, for example, public assistance benefit is not taxed. Much of this 'hidden' welfare, however, benefits middle-income people: for example, tax deductions on mortgage interest for home-owners cost the government $25 billion in lost revenue in 1985 – about double what was paid out in the same year in housing assistance for low-income people. Big business also benefited from tax exemptions. In 1985, for example, the United States federal government gave $1.9 billion to aid industry in covering costs of exploration and depletion of oil and gas resources. This was $400 million more than was spent in the same year on the nutritional programme for low-income women and children. Between 1981 and 1985 the taxes of poor people went up five times in proportion to their total income while taxes on middle and upper incomes fell (*New York Times*, 12 December 1985). Changes in 1986 mean that the situation is now more complex. Taxes on the poor have been reduced and tax exemptions benefiting the wealthy have been reduced or eliminated. However, at the same time the highest marginal rate of income tax has been cut from 50 per cent to 28 per cent. Beckman's calculations in 1985 probably best sum up what the changes in tax and tax exemptions in the United States under Reagan have achieved: '[the]...tax system has probably become tilted towards the 'regressive' end of the scale in recent years, especially because of the rise in social security taxes and a decline in income tax on corporations and the affluent' (1985, p. 23).

The main cuts in spending have hit welfare payments to the poor, non-contributory means-tested benefits such as Medicaid, Aid to Families with Dependent Children and food stamps. It is in this aspect of Reagan's policies that the objectives of the economic New Right and the 'moral' New Right come together. It is argued that the growth of single-parent families, male unemployment and so on are a direct consequence of the growth of the welfare state.

Many of the family's historical responsibilities have been taken over by the State ... the strength of American society has come from families' awareness that they are working together and helping one another.

Parents took care of their own children ... What might be called the modern welfare state has removed much of that awareness of loving and being loved and working together and has removed much of the sense of responsibility ... it is not surprising that as government expenditure on social welfare increases, our concerns over the family and who is taking care of the nation's children has also increased ... We must restore the American family to self-sufficiency. (Denton, 1982, p. 5)

Not only have the New Right advocated the reduction of welfare payments; they have also argued that recipients should work for benefit or be forced into low-paid jobs. 'The solution must be in public authority. Low wage work apparently must be mandated. Authority achieves compliance more efficiently than benefits ... Government need not make the desired behaviour worthwhile. It simply threatens punishment (in this case the loss of benefits) if they do not comply' (Mead, 1986, pp. 84–5).

Kaus (1986) argued that all social welfare benefit for the poor should be abolished and replaced by a sub-minimum waged job:

Workfare should not be short-term programs to existing welfare clients, but a long-term program to destroy the culture of poverty. In this 'hard' view what's most important is not whether sweeping streets or cleaning kitchens helps Betsy Smith, single teenage parent and high-school drop-out, learn skills that will help her find a private-sector job. It is whether the prospect of sweeping streets or cleaning kitchens for welfare grant will deter Betsy Smith from having the illegitimate child that drops her out of school and onto welfare in the first place – or finding that the *sight* of Betsy Smith sweeping streets after having had her illegitimate child will discourage her younger sisters and neighbours from doing as she did. (p. 27)

Ronald Reagan, when he came to office, shared the views of not only the Christian but also the economic New Right. Welfare spending was inflationary, diverted resources from private sector investment and encouraged dependency and also immoral behaviour by making single motherhood a viable alternative. While the economic New Right were more concerned about reducing government spending, the 'moral' and Christian New Right were more concerned with 'moral' issues, specifically those designed to reinforce the traditional patriarchal nuclear family. However, this family was seen also as the basis for a strong capitalist society because it forced men to work hard for their families. While a policy objective of preventing women's access to abortion and then barring them from state income maintenance might appear contradictory, in fact they were both aimed at discouraging single women from engaging in sex and getting pregnant. The aim was to encourage moral behaviour. However, as we have seen, from the evidence of Reagan's achievement in the area of 'moral' reform he placed more emphasis on economic reforms during his administration. In 1981 he argued:

> Our society's commitment to an adequate social safety net contains powerful, unhealthy expansionary tendencies. If left unchecked these forces threaten eventual fiscal ruin and serious challenges to basic social values of independence and self support. The Federal Government has created so many entitlements for unnecessary benefits that it is essential to begin paring back. (quoted in Currie and Skolnick, 1988, p. 116)

The United States has never had a welfare state comparable to that found in Britain. During the 1960s there was an expansion of policy to help the poor. However, even then public assistance programmes accounted for less than two per cent of GNP, and the ratio of public assistance to earnings of unskilled manual workers has remained constant with the 1950 figure of between 25 and 30 per cent. In 1978, public spending on income support was 10 per cent of GNP – 75 per cent of this being spent on 'social insurance' programmes – that is, Social Security, Medicare, unemployment compensation and disability-related programmes. Even before Reagan came to office 'the United States's notoriously stingy system of income support helped give [us] the highest rates of family and child poverty in the advanced industrial world' (Currie, 1990, p. 304).

The main cutbacks under Reagan have been in the income maintenance programmes, in terms both of levels of benefit and of coverage. In Reagan's first term the percentage of unemployed receiving benefits fell by a third, and the Trade Assistance Act which enabled special employment benefit and the Employment and Job Training funds were cut. Rent subsidies for the poor and funds for the rehabilitation of low-income housing were reduced. Cuts also were made in the funding for Aid for Families with Dependent Children, food stamps and Medicaid. The total reduction in these programmes was $57 billion, representing a third of all federal cuts, in programmes that only accounted for a tenth of the federal budget.

While these cuts were being made in welfare spending, the number of people living below the official poverty line rose from 26 million to 35 million and the number of children in poverty increased. Poor families became poorer. In 1983, 42 per cent of the 13 million poor children lived in families with an income below 50 per cent of the poverty line. At the same time rich families became better off. Ten per cent of families increased their income by an average of $5,000+

(allowing for inflation) from 1980 to 1984 (Ehrenreich and Fox Piven, 1984). Those families most likely to be living in poverty were single-parent families, mainly headed by a female. In 1984, 9 million white children and 5 million black children lived with a single parent – 21 per cent of all children. Women and their dependent children were the single largest group of poor in the United States. They formed over 80 per cent of all Aid to Families with Dependent Children recipients, over half of all those who received food stamps, 55 per cent of all households receiving Medicaid, well over half of non-waged residents of public housing and 50 per cent of receivers of free or reduced-price school meals (Rodgers, 1986).

The number of female-headed families has increased rapidly in the United States because of high divorce rates and increases in the number of women who choose to have babies outside of marriage. The unemployment/non-employment rate for female heads of household is high – in 1984, 66.3 per cent were not economically active. Even those who are in employment are likely to be in low-paid jobs. Those who are not in employment are dependent on the welfare benefits that have been most severely cut under Reagan, so that they and their children are likely to be living on or below the poverty line; the vast majority of female-headed families with no income other than AFDC live below the poverty line (Rodgers, 1986).

Aid for Families with Dependent Children (AFDC) has declined in value in real terms under Reagan – although the decline began before Reagan came into office. Between 1970 and 1984 average welfare benefit for poor families with children fell by a third (House Ways and Means Committee, 1985). In 1981 budget changes both reduced the incomes of welfare-dependent families and excluded some families from benefits altogether. Food stamps are redeemable only for food, but because they are means-tested they overcome some of the inequalities in AFDC between states. In 1981 Congress voted to allow states to count food stamps benefit as income, thereby reducing the possibility of AFDC cash payment. New rules on 'earnings disregards' and costs of employment that could be deducted from earnings in calculating benefit entitlement meant that many mothers in low-paid employment were excluded from AFDC (Kammerman, 1984, p. 252). The overall funding for AFDC payments declined in real terms from 1975 onwards (House Ways and Means Committee, 1985, p. 252). The House Select Committee on Hunger (1985) found that because of cutbacks in AFDC, food stamps and school lunch programmes, over one-third of the gains made against hunger and malnutrition in the 1960s and 1970s had been wiped out. The total benefit payable to poor families is very low – the state average for a family of four in 1986 was 65 per cent of the official poverty line and was only above 65 per cent in a quarter of the states (Edelman, 1987; Ellwood, 1988). Yet the combined value of AFDC and food stamps had been cut by 20 per cent between 1971 and 1986 while the proportion of poor children receiving these benefits dropped from 72 per cent to 60 per cent (US Congress, 1988; Ellwood and Summers, 1986). Between 1975 and 1983 the purchasing power of welfare fell by 30 per cent.

The other aim of the Reagan administration was to force those on welfare into work unless they were disabled or sick. The 1981 legislation did not require states to introduce 'workfare' – that is, the idea of working for one's benefits – but it gave them power to do so. The requirement to engage in work-related programmes could be extended to lone mothers with children aged 3 to 5 years, as long as child care was provided. Clearly the measure was aimed at eliminating welfare dependency. However, only 26 states introduced these programmes.

In 1984 Congress passed legislation requiring the states to establish a system for ensuring that biological fathers paid child support. States were required to deduct child support payment from wages after one month's default. All states were required to set standards for the amount of child support fathers should be obliged to pay (Corbett, 1985). This is a further measure aimed at reducing what is seen as 'welfare dependency' but also one that reinforces the importance of the biological family and parental responsibility.

In February 1986 Reagan announced that his administration would bring forward proposals for reforming welfare. Influenced by the work of Charles Murray (see Chapter 5), he argued that there was a growing class of welfare recipients made up of single parent families and residents of the inner cities. He maintained that the existing welfare system did little to help the poor become self-sufficient. However, the proposals in the Family Support Act of 1988 are very limited despite the claim that it aims 'to ensure that needy families with children obtain the education, training and employment that will help them avoid long term welfare dependency' (Human Services, 8 October 1988, 2826). In fact it is a continuation of existing policies – cuts in welfare and attempts to enforce workfare even for mothers with young children and to oblige the biological fathers to pay child support. As Yasmine Ergas (1990) says, its implicit attempt is 'to reconstruct the parental couple as the fulcrum of family organisation' (p. 2). Thus the act focuses largely on single-parent families, which the New Right have portrayed as the major threat to the 'traditional' family and to the economic strength of the United States – by encouraging men's irresponsibility, crime, drug abuse and unemployment. However, the emphasis on reducing 'welfare dependency' in the act not only reinforces the notion of the two-parent family by attempting to reinforce parental child welfare payment but attacks the New Right belief that young children need to be cared for by their mothers. Women with children aged 3 to 5 years can be required to participate in workfare programmes. At the same time, state day-care centres for children were closed, so that mothers would have to find the cost of childcare while they went to work. This devalues the ideal of motherhood and the idea that childcare is work for women. It is justified on the grounds that young unmarried women need to have the discipline imposed by work outside the home (presumably because they do not have a husband to discipline them at home). However, divorced women equally are forced into work by the provisions of the act. There seems to be a real contradiction between policies advocated by the economic New Right and those of the moral New Right in this respect – although this could also be seen by the moral New Right as an incentive not to get pregnant in the first place.

The Family Support Act shows that Reagan's major concerns were with reducing welfare spending and eliminating what was seen by the economic New Right as welfare dependency. 'At the policy level, the Reaganites not only eliminated some programmes and cut others but precluded further advances in the social welfare area for the foreseeable future '(Currie and Skolnick, 1988, p. 167). Poverty increased under Reagan, as did the gap between rich and poor. Policies aimed at reducing welfare dependency were targeted especially at single-parent families, who have been greatly disadvantaged by cuts in welfare spending. However, 'research does not support the view that welfare encourages two-parent family break up' and the availability of welfare 'has little impact on the child bearing rates of unmarried women' (report of the US General Accounting Office, released 22 March 1987, quoted in Ehrenreich, 1987). Ellwood and Summers (1986, p. 96) maintain 'It is true that current transfer policies do little to help the poor achieve self-sufficiency or to ameliorate some of the serious social problems attending poverty, but a review of the record does not support the view that they have caused them.' Edelman (1987) argues that 'both public and private sector neglect and anti-family policy have contributed to a downward spiral for families and children, black and white' (p. 23).

Housing also became more problematic for families under Reagan, with an increasing gap between those who own their own houses and those seeking adequate housing. Rising house prices have made it difficult for young and low-income families to buy their own houses. There have also been severe cuts in the rudimentary US system of public housing; low-income housing programmes have been drastically cut. Between 1976 and 1982 federal subsidies and tax incentives helped support the construction of about 200,000 units of low-cost housing a year for those on low incomes. By the late 1980s this had fallen to 25,000 – mainly for the old and disabled (Connell, 1988, p. 6). There have also been cuts in funding to maintain and improve public housing, cuts in funding for public housing conversions, and the conversion of many public units into private ones, forcing many low-income households into a private housing market which has seen rents rise dramatically in the 1980s. The result is a dramatic rise in homelessness and an increased burden of housing costs, especially among the bottom fifth of income earners, where the median rent burden went up by one-third between 1974 and 1987. For those households with children, it rose by 50 per cent (Joint Center for Housing Studies, 1988, p. 14).

Conclusion

These results indicate that family poverty has increased in the US and that Reagan's policies did little to alleviate it. According to Edelman (1987), nearly half of all black children and one-sixth of white children are poor – that is, there are 8.1 million poor white children and 4.3 million poor black children. Thus, more than 20 per cent of all children and nearly 25 per cent of children under six years of age live in poverty in the United States. Reagan's policies have done little to alleviate this or to support families and family life. A substantial proportion of married and non-married women with children, including pre-school children, have paid employment in the United States. The decline in real incomes in the 1980s means that many families need two wages to have a decent standard of living, and the low level of welfare benefits forces many single-parent mothers into employment – often low-paid, given the gender-segregated nature of the labour market. Women with young children can also get tax relief on child care costs – a further inducement to work – although public day-care centres have been closed down, and tax relief can be claimed only retrospectively and advantages high-income families most .

In America under Reagan, few of the policies of the pro-family movement were implemented. Nor did the traditional two-parent patriarchal family consistently benefit from economic policies. However, the attack on the economic well-being of single-parent families has been much more severe in the United States than in Britain. Also, the 'moral' and Christian New Right have had a much higher profile in the US than in Britain and have organised a large and vocal extra-governmental lobby which has given much greater prominence to pro-family ideas.

7

Putting Ideas into Practice (2): The Pro-Family Movement and Social Policy in Britain under the Thatcher Administration

In Britain the pro-family movement has been closely identified with Mrs Thatcher and the Conservative administration that took power in 1979. There has been no strong extra-parliamentary New Right 'pro-family' movement as in the US. The extra-parliamentary New Right has in the main been restricted to a small number of 'think tanks' and academies more concerned with economic policies than with morals. Although the Conservative Party under Mrs Thatcher expressed a commitment to 'pro-family' ideas and to reforms aimed at strengthening 'the family', domestic, economic and foreign policies seem to have received more attention than social policy, especially in Mrs Thatcher's first term.

The Conservative administration under Margaret Thatcher's leadership developed no explicit family policy but did endorse a particular image of 'the family'. The Conservative Party regards itself as 'the party of the family'. In its 1983 Party manifesto, for example, five 'great tasks' were identified, one of which was 'to build a responsible society which protects the weak but allows the family and the individual to flourish'. Mrs Thatcher also made it clear that her policies should be judged against their impact on families: 'We shall judge these policies by one simple test: do they make life better for individuals and their families?' (New Year Message, 30 December 1983).

It is clear that this Conservative support is for a particular form of family – 'the family' of the New Right pro-family movement. This view of the family, deriving from Christian morality, is that it should be based upon marriage: 'The family is founded by the institution of marriage which is a union for life and is the vital link which binds together the family' (Conservative Political Centre, 1981: 28). Furthermore, in the view of some Conservatives, it is a family where wives are economically dependent upon husbands: 'Quite frankly, I don't think that mothers have the same right to go to work as fathers do. If the good Lord had intended us to have equal rights to go out to

117

work he would not have created men and women. These are biological facts' (Jenkins, 1977). We should note here, however, the contradictions between the traditional idea of the patriarchal family and the libertarian individualist tradition which would see women as being free to choose to work (see Chapter 1).

It is agreed that parents are responsible for socialising and disciplining their children – 'It is at home that children first learn right from wrong' (speech by Mrs Thatcher, 1985) – and it is because of the failure of families to do so that there are so many social problems: 'The origins of crime lie deep in society: in families where parents do not support or control their children ... ' (Conservative Party Manifesto, 1987, p. 55). The problems of the inner city, it appears, will be solved not only by government spending but ' by giving back personal responsibility (through ownership), security (through law and order) and stability (through strengthening a sense of personal obligation, most notably within families) ' (Tebbit, 1985). Perhaps the 'pro-family' idea of the family has been most clearly expressed by the Conservative Family Campaign, a pressure group within the Conservative Party concerned that party policy should support 'the family'. While at one level this organisation can be seen as critical of the Thatcher administration, being forced to campaign for the Conservative Party to put 'the family' at the top of its agenda, it nevertheless is supported by a number of influential Conservatives both in and outside of Parliament. Furthermore, its 'pro-family' agenda clearly summarises what was suggested by the Conservative Party in the 1980s. It argues for:

1. The support of the family in public policy.
2. The acceptance by the Conservative Party of the defence of the family as a central policy issue.
3. The upholding of Christianity as the faith of the nation and the reflection of its values in law and education.
4. A complete overhaul of the tax and Social Security system to ensure that marriage and the family are supported and strengthened.
5. The radical reform of laws governing abortion, divorce, obscenity and other issues affecting the family. (Graham Webster-Gardiner and Stephen Green, 1988 CFC publicity leaflet)

Underlying the Conservative view of the family are three clear ideas. First, a particular form of the family – the patriarchal, nuclear family – is natural and God-given. Second, this particular kind of family is under attack. Third, the decline of 'the family' threatens the stability of the nation – 'the family' being the basic building block of the British nation.

The key question is the extent to which the Thatcher administration actually created the family of the New Right ideology. Has the government actively sought to remoralise society, reduce welfare dependency and support the family? Soon after the Conservative Party came into office a Family Policy Group was established chaired by Ferdinand Mount, then a policy adviser to Mrs Thatcher. The committee was made up of key members of the Conservative government of the time: Geoffrey Howe (Chancellor of the Exchequer), Keith Joseph (Minister of Education), Micheal Heseltine (Minister of the Environment), Patrick Jenkins (Minister for Industry), David Howell (Minister for Transport), Norman Fowler (Minister for Health and Social Security), Norman Tebbit (Minister for Employment), Timothy Raison (Home Office Minister) and John Sparrow (one of the Central Policy Review Staff). The policies suggested by this group demonstrate clearly the interlinking in New Right thought of the idea of the family, the concern for individual freedom and the concern with cutting back state spending and intervention in the economy. A number of the recommendations clearly demonstrated their views on family and family life. They thought that mothers with young children should be encouraged to stay at home, that financial disincentives against motherhood should be removed to facilitate this, and that the tax/benefits system should be oriented more towards the family. However, they also suggested that the family, in the widest sense, should be encouraged to take on responsibility for the disabled, the elderly and unemployed 16-year-olds. Furthermore, they felt that consideration should be given to determining if the present benefits for single mothers struck the correct balance between support and providing incentives for self-reliance. Parents, they felt, should take more responsibility for their children and have more involvement in schools. They should also take on responsibility for their children's anti-social behaviour. The group advocated the introduction of educational vouchers, the establishment of more religious schools and more help for parents who wanted to set up schools. They felt that education should teach self-reliance, responsibility, a capacity for enterprise and positive attitudes towards work. Schools and banks should provide schemes to encourage children to save their pocket money and encourage more positive attitudes towards wealth creation.

They argued that professionals such as teachers and social workers undermine individual self-respect. They suggested competition between services and that services should be provided in such a way that they did not erode individual self-respect. They suggested more private provision for social needs (but with the state providing a basic minimum safety net) to encourage private pensions, the voluntary sector and charitable giving. The government, they suggested, should increase incentives to employment by, for example, curbing the Wages Councils (which set minimum wage-rates in some industrial sectors) and by reducing regulation on smaller firms. They suggested lowering the taxation burden at the lower end and encouraging home ownership. They thought that government equal opportunities policy should concentrate upon emphasising the ways in which self-reliance and self-help enabled people to be upwardly mobile, quoting the example of Asian shopkeepers. They also thought that the government should consider the possibility of reducing pornography and television and press violence (*Guardian*, 17 February 1983). This report laid down many of the principles for reform that informed the radical policies of the Thatcher administration.

Moral Policies

The British government has done little to reform – in a more conservative direction – the so-called permissive legislation of the 1960s and 1970s. Divorce actually has become simpler, not more difficult, and the divorce rate has continued to rise steadily in the last ten years. The Matrimonial Proceedings Act of 1984, introduced by the Conservatives, allows people to petition for divorce after the first anniversary of marriage instead of waiting for three years, and this led to 191,000 divorce petitions being filed in 1985 – a 6 per cent increase over 1984. Other legislation introduced under the Conservatives recognises the rights of 'illegitimate' heirs. The laws on homosexuality and pornography have remained virtually unchanged, and while a number of Private Members' Bills have attempted to reform the 1967 Divorce Law Reform Act and the 1968 Abortion Reform Act, none of them has been successful or been taken up as a Government Bill. (An exception was the amendment to the Human Life and Embryo Protection Act 1990 which reduced the time limit for abortion from 28 to 24 weeks.) The number of married women in paid employment outside the home has increased steadily, at least partly as an indirect consequence of government economic policies encouraging the re-structuring of industry and the creation of low-paid part-time jobs.

However, there have been some measures that might be seen as explicitly pro-family. The Education Reform Act 1988 gave increased control to parents over their children's schooling, required that sex education be taught in the context of the heterosexual, nuclear family, that religious education taught in schools was mainly Christian and that school assemblies were mainly or wholly Christian. (See also Clause 29 of the Local Government Act 1988, which prevents local authorities from 'promoting homosexuality'.) These were all issues which were specifically targeted by the Conservative Family

Campaign, as we saw in Chapter 3. In practice, however, Clause 29 has not been as draconian in its implications as was originally feared by its opponents (Evans, 1989). Small victories for the 'Moral' Right arising from Clause 29 included the removal of *Jenny Lives with Eric and Martin* (the story of a small girl brought up by a homosexual couple) from the library shelves in Wolverhampton, the decision of the Hereford and Worcester Council to refuse to a lesbian group a grant to print material, the decision by Brighton Workers' Educational Association (a voluntary organisation providing non-vocational evening classes) to change the name of a 'lesbian literature' course, and the decision by the Southampton Council to drop a chapter on lesbianism from a Women's Handbook. Hardly overwhelming!

The temporary victory of Victoria Gillick – who fought against a doctor's decision to give the contraceptive pill to her daughter, who was below the age of 16, without first having her or her husband's consent – was seen as a victory for the Moral Right. Mrs Gillick was indeed a veteran campaigner on moral issues. This decision won in the Higher Court would have applied to all girls below the age of 16 had it not been reversed on appeal. However, this could also be seen as a final victory for the medical profession to control the lay person rather than for the rights of young women over their own sexuality, because only medical practitioners can make decisions to break the law by prescribing the contraceptive pill for an under-aged girl – see David (1986). Furthermore, many feminists would agree with Victoria Gillick that the contraceptive pill also can be used to put young women under pressure to provide sexual access to men, and so the issue is not a simple or clear-cut one. This is one of many examples of women in the 'moral' New Right becoming leading spokespeople over issues affecting female sexuality. It is an issue we address in the final chapter.

Economic Policies

In terms of income maintenance – by which we mean both social security and taxation – the record of the government is also mixed with respect to the ways in which policies have contributed to the objectives of the pro-family movement. Some measures could be seen as pro-family or as promoting family values, while other changes have not resulted in clearly advantaging the heterosexual nuclear family over other domestic units. Key examples of 'pro-family' measures would be the tightening up of eligibility for income maintenance, especially for married women claiming unemployment benefit (a universal benefit paid to those with a specified contribution record). This means that, when claiming benefit, women with children under school age have to specify the arrangements they have made for child care if they were to get a job. They must do this in order to meet the criteria of being 'genuinely available for work' – though unemployed men with young children are not required to do the same. The unemployed have also been forced to state that they will be prepared to take a job anywhere in the country – a difficult condition for married women (and indeed men) with dependent children. These measures have been largely symbolic in their impact rather than serving to actually prevent most eligible women from claiming benefit. Probably the main group excluded are married women who have exhausted maternity benefit and have not yet returned to paid employment, because they are the ones most likely to be questioned about childcare arrangements.

There also has been a change in the eligibility of young people for income maintenance. From April 1988, young people aged 16 to 18 were no longer entitled to income support (a non-contributory benefit paid on the basis of a means test), except in cases of exceptional need. This was in fact the sixteenth cut in benefits to young people since 1980 (Randall, 1989, p. 5). Instead, they are expected to take up places in the Youth Training (YT) scheme (a two-year scheme to train young people for work, under which they receive an allowance) if they do not stay in education or obtain employment on the open market. Those who do not or cannot avail themselves of this scheme must remain dependent on their parents. The latter are no longer entitled to Child Benefit, which ceases when a child leaves full-time education. The allowances paid on YT are very low, certainly insufficient to enable young people to live independently and probably insufficient for them to maintain themselves even if they remain in the parental home. Under the 1986 Social Security Act, benefit levels for 18 to 25 year olds are lower than those paid to people over 25 in the same circumstances, although an exception is made for young people over 18 with children. This makes young people increasingly dependent upon their parents. There has been a considerable rise in homelessness and destitution amongst young people. A National Association of Citizens' Advice Bureaux (NACAB) Report in 1989 found increasing numbers of young people homeless and unable, for a variety of reasons, to return to their parental home. They also found that families were increasingly facing the alternative of getting into debt or requiring their son or daughter to leave home.

Not only are families expected to care economically and socially for young people, but also for other dependents. Policies of community care mean that families are expected to care for their elderly and handicapped members. 'If we are to maintain, let alone extend, the level and standard of care in the community we must first try to put responsibility back where it belongs, with the family and with people themselves' (Thatcher, 1977, p. 83)

The influential White Paper *Caring for People* (Department of Health, 1990) makes it clear that the government expect families to provide care with little financial or professional support. The Community Charge (a flat-rate tax for financing local government) introduced in Scotland in 1989 and England and Wales in 1990 also increased the financial burden on families caring for elderly or handicapped relatives as well as those with young people over the age of 18 still living in the parental home. Furthermore, it financially disadvantaged the traditional nuclear family, because the Community Charge of a non-employed wife had to be paid by her husband.

As soon as they came into office, Mrs Thatcher's administration cut welfare benefits in real terms. The initial attack was on the insurance-based and means-tested benefits. The 1980 Social Security Act legislated for benefit increases to be tied to prices rather than wages. Benefit levels in real terms have fallen significantly in relation to wages. In 1982 under the 1980 Act, earnings-related unemployment and maternity benefits were abolished and benefits became taxable. Unemployment and other short-term benefits were also cut by 5 per cent. According to an analysis in *The Times* in 1981, within the first two years of the Thatcher administration the total value of state support for an unemployed couple with two children had fallen by 40 per cent (Novak, 1988). The 1980 Education Act abolished the requirement for schools to provide lunches except for those entitled to free meals, eligibility for free meals was reduced, and the local educational authorities were required to charge the economic cost of a meal. Also, the government tightened up entitlement to single payments under the social security legislation for one-off large essential items and virtually abolished clothing grants for families on supplementary benefits.

In terms of income maintenance and tax, it was pointed out in the mid-1980s that at about every stage of life a married couple with children were at a tax and welfare disadvantage when compared with single parents, co-habiting couples and homosexual households (Parker, 1986). The number of families headed by someone earning a wage below the poverty line increased by nearly a fifth between 1979 and 1985 (DHSS 1988).

By 1985 four million people in families with children (16 per cent of all families with children) lived at or below the poverty line. This was a two-fold increase since 1979. Two and a quarter million, 18 per cent of all children, were living in poverty – a 9 per cent increase since 1979. Nearly six and a half million people in families with children, 26 per cent of all such families, were living in or on the margins of poverty – a 55 per cent increase since 1979 (Low Pay Unit, 1988).

The Fowler Review of Social Security carried out in 1985 and subsequently resulting in legislation (in 1986) was more concerned with redistributing benefits amongst the poor than with supporting traditional families. However, the 1988 Budget reformed the tax system so that on the whole the so-called 'tax on marriage' has been eliminated. The 'tax on marriage', as the Conservative Family Campaign called it, meant that a married couple was treated less favourably than a co-habiting couple under taxation laws. This ignores the fact that co-habiting couples are treated less favourably under social security if the male partner dies – that is, there is no entitlement to widow's benefits or to a pension based on the male partner's contributions. The changes meant that mortgage interest tax relief could only be claimed on a property, not by individuals, so that married couples who under the old system could only claim one tax relief were no longer at a tax disadvantage. Co-habiting couples can now only claim an additional tax allowance for one child – giving them exactly the same tax relief as a married couple where the husband can claim for his wife (or the wife for her husband). The separate taxation of wives introduced in 1990 mainly advantages better-off married couples who have investment income. Married women are able to use their own tax allowance against their unearned income; in the past, it was added to the husband's income and taxed at his highest marginal tax rate. The changes do not in the main affect married women in employment, who previously had a married woman's tax allowance equal to that of a single person. High-earning couples, who became liable to higher rates of tax when their incomes were aggregated, could always apply for separate assessment to reduce tax liability.

However, while these changes remove some of the advantages of co-habiting couples over married couples, they do not specifically help the family where mother stays at home to care for young children. Such families only receive the same tax allowances as the family where both parents decide to go out to work or where a couple co-habit rather than get married.

The 1985 Fowler Review of Social Security was undertaken to reform and simplify the social security system. It was also designed to ensure that the cost of social security did not increase and to differentiate more strongly between the deserving and undeserving poor. The stated aim was: ' ... first ... to provide help for families generally whilst the second is to provide extra help for low income families' (*Reform of Social Security*, Vol. 2, p. 48). Furthermore, it said: 'Families whose needs are likely to be greatest ... may be defined as those falling within the bottom 20 per cent of the distribution of national income with family incomes being adjusted for differences in family size to allow for the greater requirements of large families' (*Reform of Social Security,* Vol. 2, p. 13).

Those most affected by poverty, it was argued, were families with children. Hence the need was to direct benefits to those families most in need and to provide better subsidies to low-paid workers in order to provide work incentives (or to reduce disincentives to work). From the moral Conservative point of view the main problem with the array of benefits available was that they meant it was possible for those out of work to be better off than those in work in very low-paid jobs. This was despite the existence of Family Income Supplement (FIS, now replaced with Family Credit), a means-tested, non-contributory benefit to make up the wages of low-income families in full-time employment to a specified amount. There was a need both to remove the poverty trap which reinforced dependence on benefits and provided a disincentive to move off benefit, and to enable men to see the full value of their income. 'The disincentives to work and self-help are exacerbated by the way that Child Benefit and FIS (Family Income Supplement) are paid normally to the wife, so that wage earners may not be fully aware of the total income their family is receiving' (Fowler Review of Social Security, 1985).

In Fowler's view, not only did men not realise the true value of their income but also their position as head of the family was challenged if they did not have total control over family income. However, in the event, the Social Security Act left Child Benefit unchanged and Family Credit, the replacement for FIS, is paid to wives as was FIS. As Carol Smart (1987) has pointed out, the tension between moral values and practical policies means that the reforms have not seriously attacked the income maintenance of single parents. Indeed, using figures based on the 1988 rates, Green and Webster-Gardiner point out in their New Right pro-family pamphlet that single parents are advantaged by the legislation and other changes. While the universal child benefit payable to all mothers did not increase from 1987 to 1988, the one-parent benefit payable to single parents in addition to child benefit was raised from £4.70 to £4.90 a week. Single parents on income support (a means-tested non-contributory form of income maintenance) received a premium of £3.70 while a married couple received not £7.40 (as might be expected) but £6.15.

Family credit is paid to families where parents are in paid employment for 24 hours or more a week but have a low income. However, only 36 per cent of families who are entitled to claim it actually do so. Single parents, according to Green and Webster-Gardiner, are given two advantages over a married couple. First, the level of earnings below which the maximum credit is paid is the same for a single-parent as a two-parent family and the maximum credit, before additions for children, is the same for a single parent as a couple. Furthermore, a single parent on income maintenance is allowed to earn £15 a week before she or he loses benefit from the outset of the claim. A married man or woman is only allowed to earn £5 a week for the first two years on benefit before benefit is lost pound for pound earned. Finally, they point out that income support rates are lower for a married couple than for single adults sharing accommodation.

Poor families are no better off under the new system – designed to target those most in need – than they were under the old system. Research using illustrative figures in 1986 suggested that a family with two children with an income of £160 or less a week would be worse off – in some cases by as much as £11 per week – because of the reduction in free school meals and housing benefit when the reforms were introduced (Hansard, 1986). Research carried out by Bradshaw and Holmes (1989) based on income support rates showed that as many as half of the unemployed families with children in their small sample would be long-run losers after the changes in income support. While some families have gained from the new regulations, others have lost, the main effect being to redistribute benefit amongst the poor. As we have already pointed out, despite the fact that 'family credit' and 'family premiums' are aimed specifically at families, they do not advantage traditional patriarchal nuclear families over other forms of family. Indeed, Green and Webster-Gardiner suggest (1988):

> The net result of the treatment by social security system of single parents has been to encourage girls to have babies outside of marriage and then to let the state take responsibility for them. The DHSS provides money to live on and local councils provide accommodation and creches and day-care facilities. It is a serious matter for Conservatives that by 'caring' in excess for those who have become single parents, we create envy from those in normal families and we create huge estates of single mothers and their children.

They go on to maintain that:

> The new rules provide a single parent's charter, yet recent research has shown that single parent households are seriously disadvantageous to children psychologically, in educational attainment and in susceptibility to becoming involved in criminal activity. So great are the problems associated with single-parent households that they should not be actively encouraged. (Green and Webster-Gardiner, p. 23)

Most single-parent families are of course founded as a result of divorce, not by single women 'choosing' single parenthood. Furthermore, life for single parents is extremely difficult; living on welfare benefits, especially for those with young children, is a constrained choice because labour market segmentation makes it impossible for most women to earn sufficient to pay for childcare and to maintain themselves and their child(ren). Indeed, the 1988 Act made this more difficult by removing the disregard of earning for childcare costs and other work-related expenses for single parents and replacing it with a flat rate disregard of £15, making it difficult for a single parent to take paid employment. (Parents in Britain are not able, as are US parents, to claim an income tax allowance for childcare costs.) More importantly, the level of income maintenance paid to all families is inadequate to maintain the 'normal' standard of living in Britain. Those dependent on the state for their support are unable to participate in the normal day-to-day activities that the majority take for granted (Townsend, 1983). Furthermore, the main disadvantage of being brought up in a single-parent household is poverty.

The 1986 Social Security Act abolished the universal Maternity Allowance and replaced it with a means-tested grant for those on benefit. It also abolished single special-needs payments and replaced them with a system of loans which have to be repaid out of benefit. The amount available for loans is cash limited and claimants have to satisfy local Department of Social Security staff that they can repay the loan. Many are deterred from applying and many applicants who apply are refused, despite the fact that they can only apply for a loan with which to purchase essentials. A survey by the Citizens Advice Bureaux (1990) found that four-fifths of unemployed applicants, four-fifths of single young applicants and one-fifth of lone parent applicants were refused a loan.

Similarly, taxation policies have not been designed unambiguously to direct resources towards the family. Since 1979 the Conservatives have reduced income tax substantially, from a standard rate of 33p in the pound to 25p, and reduced the higher tax bands to a single rate of 40p in the pound. However, they have also raised National Insurance contributions and Value Added Tax (VAT). The net result has been to increase the percentage tax on the lowest paid and to decrease it for the highest paid. The hardest hit of all is the married man with two children on half the national average male earning. His tax and National Insurance contributions increased by 163 per cent between 1978 and 1987-8, compared with a 1 per cent increase for a man on average earnings and a 21 per cent decrease for a man earning ten times the national average. When other factors such as VAT, the Community Charge and the imputed value of government spending on services, health and benefits are taken into account, a similar picture emerges. The income shared by the bottom 20 per cent of households has declined by 9 per cent and that of the bottom 40 per cent by 7 per cent, whereas the income of the top 40 per cent of households has increased by 3 per cent and that of the top 20 per cent by 6 per cent (Byrne, 1987). Thus while in 1978–9 the average family with two children paid only 35 per cent of its income in taxes and national insurance contributions, in 1988–9 they paid 37.3 per cent. Furthermore, 1.6 million families with children – about 24 per cent of all families with children – have incomes too low to pay tax (*Hansard*, 23 January 1989)

Housing policy has also failed to meet the needs of many families. The emphasis on home ownership has left many unable to meet mortgage repayments; mortgage foreclosures have more than quadrupled since 1979 (Office of Population Census and Surveys 1988). Building societies repossessed nine times as many houses for mortgage default in 1987 as in 1979, and serious mortgage arrears increased by nearly six times in the same period (Malpass 1990). This, together with the sale of council housing and spiralling costs of private-sector rented housing – now de-regulated in order to remove protection for tenants and free the market – has left many families homeless; at Christmas 1987 it was estimated that 250,000 children were without homes (Brimacombe, 1987). The Conservatives extended the 'Right to Buy' scheme to make it compulsory in all Local Authority areas in 1980, with the result that over one million council houses have been sold and the total number of council houses available has fallen in each subsequent year.

In other areas, the government's attempts to reduce spending on welfare benefits have reduced the ability of families to provide for themselves. Cuts in educational spending have meant that schools need to rely increasingly on parents for the provision of books and equipment and that parents need to pay for 'extras' such as music, swimming lessons and field trips. Similar cuts in the real level of the student grants have put an additional burden on parents. Reductions in health and social service spending also put pressure on families, with longer queues and waiting lists and a lack of beds and other resources for operations. Prescription charges, for example, increased by 1100 per cent between 1979 and 1988 along with increased charges for spectacles and dental care, thus creating further economic burdens for families. Children under 16 and young people in non-higher education are exempt from these charges, as are those on state benefits and low incomes. However, they still increase the cost of living for others – and they particularly hit families if their income is too far above the means-tested level for a reduction or exemption from charges.

Rather than the family being proudly autonomous, we can see that its roles and relations, its responsibilities and tasks, and most of all its finances are determined (although mostly indirectly) by state policy. Moreover, it appears to us that, despite the arguments of the Moral Right and the way in which this discourse was used by Mrs Thatcher, the policies of familial responsibility have largely been taken on board as a means of saving money rather than moral concern.

While Mrs Thatcher appeared to share both the concern of the Moral Right over the apparent failure of the patriarchal family to assert itself and the traditional conservative view that the family is a basic building block of society, her policies did little in practice to change the ways in which the state relates to families. Many policies have continued to prioritise the heterosexual nuclear family and in some cases to reinforce the view that this is the only morally correct living arrangement, thus supporting familial ideology. However, the necessity to strengthen the family's sense of responsibility for its own welfare, by reducing intervention by and reliance on the welfare state, has been accompanied by a reduction in the economic ability of many families to do just that. Many families and individuals have had their ability to care for themselves *reduced*, not increased, by Thatcherite policies: the choices available to families are determined by income, which for many families has been reduced in real terms.

Thatcherite policies have been criticised both by the Moral Right, for failing to 'bring back' the patriarchal family, and by centre and left, for increasing the economic and social burdens placed on families. Feminists, gay groups, and the libertarian left have been more critical still; they argue that Thatcherite policies have reduced individual choices by asserting that there is only one acceptable domestic living arrangement and continuing to assume (as previous governments have done) that people not only *do* live in nuclear families but *ought* to do so. Alternative ways of living become difficult to pursue because of the ways in which familial ideology is constantly reinforced, making alternative living arrangements seem not only less desirable but deviant or even morally wrong.

Under the Thatcher administration the main outcome was the polarisation between the poor and the better off. In the eleven years of her administration a fall in the value of social security and the privatisation of housing made it more problematic for the less well-off members of society to support themselves and their families. The poor were unable to share in the activities of everyday life which the rest of the population take for granted. A recent study of families living in poverty, undertaken by the Child Poverty Action Group, concluded:

> The picture which emerges from this detailed study of family lives is one of constant restriction in almost every aspect of people's activities ... The lives of these families and perhaps most seriously, the lives of the children in them, are marked by the unrelieved struggle to manage, with dreary diets and drab clothing. They also suffer what

amounts to virtual imprisonment in their home in our society in which getting out depends upon having money to spend ... Clearly the level of benefit is not enough to allow ordinary families to share in conventional living standards. (Bradshaw and Holmes, 1989, pp. 138–9)

The realities of living in poverty in Britain in the late 1980s are clearly expressed by the parents in Mike Hardy's study (1990). One single parent explained:

It is a struggle every day. I have to shop locally because I cannot afford the bus fares to the big stores which are cheaper. I try to provide good food for the kids, but that costs more so by the end of the month we can be down to cheese on toast because I get stale bread cheap. I often go without myself because you have to feed the kids. I don't smoke, drink or go out much, but I still have to worry about a knock on the door that might mean the electric people are trying to cut me off again. There are no jobs round here and no nurseries so I can see no way out. What makes me angry is that people think you are a scrounger and living it up on benefit. In fact, I can't give my kids the kind of life I think they are entitled to. (p. 8)

A 'moral' agenda was implemented under Thatcherism, but it was not one explicitly concerned with improving the living conditions of families or even of consistently prioritising the needs of the patriarchal nuclear family. Rather, it has been concerned with constructing a new form of citizenship – active individualism that places the emphasis on individuals being resourceful in providing for their own welfare and that of others. Its primary aim is to remove what the New Right see as the 'dependency culture', or what Mrs Thatcher referred to as the 'nanny state'. As Desmond King argues: 'The New Right advocates seek not only to revise the role of the market mechanism and to end collective state policy, but also to destroy citizenship rights established during the last two centuries' (1987, p. 3).

The main thrust of this set of policies has been to reduce rights to income maintenance and other state benefits and services and to encourage people into taking low-paid, often unpleasant, employment in a context in which the commitment to full employment set out in the 1944 Employment White paper has been eroded. The emphasis has been on what is expected of individuals rather than on the rights of citizens and their families in a welfare state.

The sense of being self-reliant, of playing a role within the family, of owning one's property, of paying one's way are all part of the spiritual ballast which maintains responsible citizenship and a solid foundation from which people look around to see what more they can do for others and for themselves. (Thatcher, 1977, p. 97)

Clearly, the influence of US New Right thinkers whom we have described in Chapter 6 can be seen here. These ideas have the effect of reducing state spending and the role of the state at the expense of the poor. This is the very antithesis of the 1940s welfare state. The emphasis is on 'encouraging' men to work harder – to support their families. The real beneficiary is capital – which benefits from low-wage labour, the hard work of employees and lower taxes on profits.

The true concern for the family under the Thatcher administration was best exemplified by two policies. One was the 1988 Immigration Act, which abolished the rights of British and long-settled Commonwealth citizens to be joined by their wives and children, and only to be allowed their entry if they could be maintained without 'recourse to public funds', defined as the main weekly means-tested benefit and accommodation under the Housing Act, 1985, Part III. Not only does this clearly question the commitment of the Thatcher administration to the well-being of families and specifically of the patriarchal nuclear family; it also suggests a prior commitment to reducing welfare spending and welfare 'dependency'. The other was the policy of allowing the real value of Child Benefit to decline. It declined as a percentage of net male earnings by 27 per cent between 1979 and 1989. Furthermore, the freezing of child benefit from 1987 to 1990, was equivalent to a cut in its real value of nearly a third. This delivered the worst blow to low-income families with one working parent and is a real attack on their standard of living. It hit mothers especially, as it reinforced their economic dependence on their husbands. It can be seen as part of a process of underscoring men's responsibilities to maintain their families – as can the measure, introduced in 1990, to force absent fathers to pay up to 50 per cent of their residual disposable income in maintenance for their children. (Presumably this measure is aimed at making it difficult for men to leave their families.)

Thus the New Right policies introduced over the last ten years have had an impact on families and have intervened in families, particularly through adjustments in the tax-benefits system. However, these interventions have not been nearly as radical as the 'moral' New Right would have liked, nor have they made families more independent and able to stand on their own feet – but they *have* made it more difficult for poorer families to survive. Indeed, more households than ever before were dependent to a greater or lesser extent on state welfare under the Thatcher administration.

8

Morality and the New Right: Towards an Alternative Morality

We have argued that two major New Right elements have influenced the pro-family rhetoric of Thatcherism and Reaganism. Both Margaret Thatcher in Britain and Ronald Reagan in the United States claimed to agree with the moral precepts put forward by the Christian New Right and to accept the free-market liberalism advocated by the economic New Right. New Right intellectuals – especially in the US – have linked the economic and moral aspects of their ideas by providing a coherent theoretical justification for cutting back state welfare. These ideas have given respectable intellectual reasons for blaming the poor for their plight and single-parent mothers in particular. Their recommendations for change have focused upon women's behaviour and the need for them to sacrifice themselves:

> She can prevent delinquency by staying at home to look after the children; she can reduce unemployment by staying at home and freeing jobs for men; she can recreate a stable family unit by becoming totally economically dependent on her husband, so that she cannot leave him. *She* is the answer. (Smart, 1984, p.136; emphasis in the original)

However, when put into practice their ideas have proved disastrous: the numbers of poor have increased while there has been no detectable change in public morality. Despite the rhetorical commitment of the administrations headed by Thatcher and Reagan to the moral agenda of the mainly Christian New Right, in practice the shift in areas of morality in both countries has been slight. In neither country have major reforms in areas such as divorce, sexuality, abortion and so on taken place, nor is there evidence of a shift to the right in public attitudes on these issues over the last ten years. However, the New Right has been able to set the agenda in these areas, so that those who disagree with their policies are put in the situation of arguing against them. This has meant that a coherent social morality as an alternative to the individualistic morality of the New Right has not been developed. The New Right has been able to build an image of those who disagree with them as being anti-family, pro-pornography, pro-teenage sex, hedonistic – in fact, immoral. Similarly, they have

132

created a new ideology of social and familial responsibility that supports the free-market liberal argument for dismantling the welfare state, and particularly certain elements of it. In doing this, they have replaced the idea of collective responsibility with individualism and individual responsibility and freedom. These ideas have popular appeal because most people do feel affection for their families, enjoy their home life and, in the words of Christopher Lasch (1977), see the family as a 'haven in a heartless world'. Furthermore, many citizens have become increasingly critical of the welfare state and the ways in which it controls their lives. The welfare state did create dependency, both in terms of excluding clients from the decision-making process and in making it difficult for those on benefit to improve their living standards. Rules and regulations placed tight controls on the lives of those on income-support programmes, for example – restrictions which were criticised by feminists and the Left before the rise of the New Right. The welfare state promoted passive rather than active citizenship; those who used welfare services felt they had little control over them. The Right appealed to these popular sentiments – as well as promising people they would have more control over their lives, they also promised them lower taxes which would give them more control over their spending.

The Right also built on the strong feeling in both Britain and the United States that a clear distinction needs to be made between the 'deserving' and the 'undeserving' poor. The undeserving poor are seen as welfare dependants and scroungers. The welfare state is seen as having contributed to this by reducing the incentives to provide for oneself and one's family. Reductions in welfare spending and the targeting of benefit to specific groups are presented as giving people more control over their lives and their earnings and providing the incentives for the 'undeserving' poor to make the necessary effort to find employment to support themselves and their families. Those arguing against the New Right have been left in the position of defending the welfare state as it existed prior to the election of the Thatcher and Reagan administrations.

We accept in principle that there will be certain groups in the population who ought to be targeted. It is necessary to examine who these groups are and what their needs are. However, this must be based upon a social morality: a morality that recognises the social causes of poverty, unemployment and deviance; one that recognises the need to adopt the position of women, children, black people, poor people and other disadvantaged groups in order to understand their plight.

However, the New Right have managed to discredit and displace the ideologies of welfarism, collectivism and collective morality. Thatcherism and Reaganism have constructed an ideology of individualism, the pleasures of private life and the economic and social benefits of a 'culture of enterprise'. In doing so they have built and developed the powerful New Right criticism of consensus, welfarism and Keynesianism and replaced them with privatisation, the rolling back of the state, incentives and competition. These ideas are presented as 'common sense', as standing to reason, as obvious to any right-thinking person. Freedom, individualism, choice, competition, consumerism and incentives replace social justice, social rights and collectivism as the key principles that underpin public policy. Society is seen as made up of autonomous individuals who have innate characteristics that must be allowed to flourish – 'men [sic] are so constructed that it is natural for them to pursue private rather than public ends' (Joseph and Sumption, 1979, p. 100). The role of government is to provide a framework and an ideological climate for individuals to pursue their ends in an orderly way. Competition, incentives and enterprise provide the framework for economic growth and prosperity which is the ultimate guarantee of 'social' security. The welfare of women and children is provided for in the patriarchal nuclear family. Charity replaces state support.

The New Right attack on the welfare state also has been sustained by those who claim that it undermines the patriarchal nuclear family, that it encourages single parenthood and divorce as well as the high taxation necessary to fund it, which forces many mothers to take full-time employment. However, as we have pointed out, welfare and other social policies of the 1980s have not resulted in a decline in single-parent families, nor have they consistently advantaged the patriarchal nuclear family. High taxation also would not seem to be a major cause of married women choosing to take employment. While economic factors, including their partners not earning a 'family wage', may be a reason for some women with children to take paid employment, others do so in order to gain some degree of economic independence, stimulate their interests and provide a break from housework (Martin and Roberts, 1984). Furthermore, our analysis of economic and welfare policies in Britain and the United States in the 1980s suggests that the main effect of these policies has been to improve the living conditions of the better off and reduce those of the poor whether or not they live in conventional families.

It is evident that the welfare and economic policies advocated by the New Right – insofar as they have been implemented by the Thatcher and Reagan administrations – have been more concerned with reasserting the rights of middle-class men and maintaining capitalism than they have been with a genuine concern for men, women and children and the quality of their lives. As Michael Rustin (1985) contends:

Arguments for restoration of market forces, for strong government and for re-establishment of traditional values in the areas of the family and sexual life were moved by real anxiety about the threats which the prosperity and characteristic claims of the post-war era posed to the prerogatives of property and to the minorities associated with its rule. (p. 10)

And Lena Dominelli (1988) has pointed out that the New Right's concern is not for children or even the men and women who live in families:

The radical right's ideological attack on the family is aimed at stemming the erosion of the family by increasing women's dependency on men and that of young people on their parents. Their anxiety on the issue is rooted in the fact that men are losing their relevance to family life if their breadwinning role is lost, and with it their control over women and children. (p. 53)

Patrick Minford (1984), a New Right economist, has clearly argued for the family as the provider of welfare:

The provision of direct social services is regarded by many as something that the family should undertake. When the state provides these services, there is serious concern that families feel morally justified in abandoning their responsibility to the state. This is an unhappy situation ... Society rightly feels that elderly parents and relatives, for example ... are the responsibility of the next of kin to help. The same is true of handicapped children. (quoted by Dominelli, 1988, p. 54)

The importance the New Right place on the patriarchal nuclear family is clearly expressed in the speeches of Graham Webster-Gardiner, chair of the Conservative Family Campaign:

When families break down it is often the state which is obliged to take over their welfare at the expense of others ... Strong families look after their own and in so doing, cut the tax bills of others ... strong families pay the tax bills which allow the government to govern, whereas broken families drain the national coffers in welfare. Policing costs diminish when parents teach their children respect for authority and the self-discipline needed to become effective adults. In contrast unmarried mothers need social workers, health visitors, welfare officers, probation officers and teachers to do the work which fathers and mothers do freely and infinitely. (speech given at the launch of the Conservative Family Campaign, 14 March 1986)

The breakdown of the family, the selfishness of women who want to have paid employment, or who do not want to remain in a relationship, or who feel that the only way they can become adults is to have a child, are blamed for society's ills and specifically for adolescent criminality and high welfare-state spending. By blaming parents and specifically women, the social, economic and political factors that underlie poverty, unemployment, crime, deviance, single parenthood, educational failure and so on are ignored. The answer to all society's ills is seen as re-constituting the patriarchal nuclear family, not reforming society. Nor should the state help and support parents in their roles. As Paul Johnson states:

> The breakdown of family life is a huge social and economic, as well as moral, evil [and] the weakness of family life in Britain is most probably the biggest single cause, not merely of habitual crime, but also of poor educational standards and so of chronic unemployment. All these evils are interconnected. The financial and economic cost is incalculable. The cost in human misery does not bear thinking about. (1987, p. 12)

Women are seen as the major cause of breakdown of individual morality and increasing welfare dependency and feminism is seen as having enticed women away from their natural duties: women, it is suggested, have sacked fathers. Either they choose to have children outside of marriage, or they fail to remain attentive to 'their man' and end up divorced. The view that it is a woman's responsibility to keep the marriage intact and to remain attractive and attentive to her husband is clearly set out in Mirabel Morgan's *The Total Woman*. In this book, she describes a programme she has developed to enable a woman to keep her man. The main emphasis is that it is a woman's responsibility to provide for her husband's needs and to remain sexually attractive to him. She quotes approvingly the words of a man who phoned in to one of her radio programmes:

> I am disgusted that Mrs Morgan didn't have problems a little bit sooner so that I could have solved my marital problems and been married today. Everything she said on the programme is exactly what took place in my marriage. I was just unable to relate to my wife or to get the point across that she was nagging and not letting me be somewhat independent, which is my nature. Had she been able to take this course, I think that today I would be happily married and be able to share the joys not only of my wife but of my child. (p. 187)

Women are therefore blamed for the breakdown in family life. This raises the question as to what evidence there is of a decline in the family and of morality. The major argument put forward by the New Right is that there has been a large increase in single-parent families, that these (mainly female-headed) families are welfare-dependent, raise children who are trapped into welfare dependency and who do not develop moral values so that they become criminals, drug addicts, prostitutes and so on. When mothers 'sack' fathers it means that men do no work and turn to a life of crime and drug addiction. There is often implicitly or explicitly a harking back to the golden age when women and children could walk the streets safely, when the strong, patriarchal Victorian family existed independently of interference by the state and when a strong morality sustained it. Whether or not Britain and the United States have become less 'moral' societies is in itself debatable. Pearson (1983) has convincingly argued that Britain in the 1980s was a more moral society than in the Victorian era. He contends that there are recurring panics about moral decline, all looking back to the golden age of harmony that never actually existed. He suggests that we now have less tolerance of crime, including violent crime, unusual sexual behaviour and abuse of children in the public and private sphere than was the case in the Victorian era. At that time, strong moral rhetoric coexisted alongside very large numbers of prostitutes and the acceptance that married men could have extra-marital sexual relations. Men could physically assault their wives without fear of punishment and young children were employed to work in the most appalling conditions. Killing someone in a street brawl often was recorded as 'causing an affray' rather than murder.

The 'cycles of disadvantage' research funded by the DHSS after Keith Joseph's speech in 1974 demonstrated, curiously, that economic factors were far more important in determining life chances than single parenthood *per se*. The unemployment of single men, especially single black men, in the United States would seem to be more a consequence of the economic situation – the lack of employment opportunities – than the fact that they are not married or are work-shy. The welfare dependency of single mothers (whether they are single as a result of divorce, desertion or never marrying) would seem to relate as much to the poverty trap created by the benefits system, the lack of affordable childcare and the segregated labour market which relegates women to low-paid jobs as to women wanting to stay on benefits (Currie, 1990). However, the criticism of single mothers for staying on benefits not only contradicts the New Right argument for motherhood but ignores the even greater burden that the double shift puts on a mother who has no one with whom to share domestic work or childcare responsibilities, however minimally.

It is also necessary to ask to what extent there *has* been a breakdown in the family. We need to recognise that a variety of family structures exist and that these change over time. There are many kinds of families rather than *the* family, and this is not simply a response to change but a recognition of what has always been – a variety of family structures. Since World War Two there has been a decline in Britain and the United States in the proportion of households that comprise nuclear families and the proportion of the total population living in nuclear families. However, this is a result of changes in population structure so that there are now more single-person and couple households. Most babies are still born into and raised in a nuclear family, and in adult life form a 'new' nuclear family. It is still seen as the norm for people to live in a nuclear family, although there have been changes in the ways in which people think that the family should be organised. In Britain and the United States it is now usual for most married women, including those with children, to have paid employment. However, the type of employment taken and the hours worked is often conditioned by their domestic and childcare responsibilities. Women do not abandon their childcare and domestic responsibilities when they take on paid employment; they try to juggle both.

The dominance of New Right ideology in the debates about family breakdown is demonstrated in the ways in which the evidence is presented. We are told how many marriages end in divorce, how many children live in single-parent families and so on. Yet we can also look at these statistics another way – to show the stability of the family. Six out of ten couples who get married in the 1990s, according to present trends, will stay together until one of them dies. Seven out of eight children are born to parents living together, three quarters of whom are legally married. Only one in five children will experience parental divorce by the time he or she is 16; that is, four out of five children born to a married couple will be brought up by them in an intact family. In 1985, 78 per cent of British children under 16 were living with both natural parents who were legally married, 9 per cent were living with one natural parent and one step-parent, 10 per cent living with a lone mother and 2 per cent living elsewhere. In all, 88 per cent of children under 16 were living in a two-parent family.

The situation in the United States is similar to that in Britain, although there is a slightly higher proportion of single-parent (mainly female-headed) families. However, as in Britain, single parenthood is a stage for many mothers rather than a permanent state. A high percentage of divorcees remarry. There is also a race difference in the United States: black children are much more likely to be in a single (mother-headed) family than white children. By the mid-1980s four out of five white children but only two out of five black children were growing up in a home with two parents (Currie and Skolnick, 1988,

p. 251). Nevertheless, only about 6 per cent of American children were living in a single-parent family at any one time.

Sociological research in Britain and the United States also challenges many of the arguments of the New Right. Satisfaction with family life has probably increased in recent years, and this appears due to greater affluence resulting in higher living standards. Men spend more time at home, and families are increasingly child-centred. Higher divorce rates may cause temporary distress and disruption but on balance have probably added to the improvement in the quality of married life, as people no longer feel compelled to stay with someone for whom they no longer care. The evidence of the effects of divorce on children is contradictory, but on balance it suggests that they suffer no long-term psychological damage. The idea that broken families are responsible for raising children without a strong morality also does not hold up to close scrutiny. It seems that it is the quality of family life not the presence of both parents that is the key factor in influencing childhood and adolescent development. This is mainly determined by the family's overall income and the availability of social and economic support.The key factor is not the presence of the father but of a viable income. The problems of single-parent families are caused by *poverty* rather than the absence of a father. As Diana Pearce puts it 'the typical outcome of a marital breakup for a family with children is that the man becomes *single* while the woman becomes *a single parent*' (Pearce, 1982, p. 12, quoted in Currie and Skolnick, 1988, p. 223; emphasis in original).

Furthermore, the New Right view of the family ignores not just the 'dark side' of family life – wife assault, wife rape, child assault and child rape – but also the domination and exploitation of women in marriage. Research by Jan Pahl (1980) and Hilary Graham (1987) has indicated that married women can be poor even within relatively affluent households because they get a small share of household resources.

The moral New Right are concerned not only with reviving the patriarchal nuclear family but with, as they see it, remoralising society. They vigorously attack welfarism, divorce, abortion and sexual deviancy. Permissiveness is seen as the main cause of contemporary social problems. The patriarchal family and a restatement of individualistic (Christian) morality play key roles. It is essential to recognise the potential appeal of arguments which simultaneously legitimate cutbacks in state welfare, placing responsibility clearly with the family, while eventually blaming liberal attitudes and legislation for today's social problems. The rhetoric of the 'moral' New Right, while combining with the liberal, free-market economic New Right in advocating cuts in public spending, does so for different reasons. It argues that Britain's decline is a result of permissiveness, a permissiveness that has undermined the foundation of society: the family. Thus the 'moral' New Right provide an ethical justification for reducing welfare spending, enforcing programmes of workfare and so on. While they proclaim the freedom of the individual and individual morality the ultimate goal is the strengthening of patriarchal capitalism, a system that systematically advantages middle-class white men and disadvantages, exploits and subordinates women, children, non-whites, the elderly, the working class and those who do not enter into heterosexual monogamous marriages.

The New Right view of the family and marriage is from the standpoint of middle-class white men, although they claim it as universal. The family helps to support and sustain patriarchal capitalism, a system that advantages white middle-class men over other groups in society. It serves their interests while disadvantaging and exploiting others. It is necessary to be aware of the site from which those who advocate the morality of the New Right are speaking, while recognising that many of the most vocal supporters of the arguments of the 'moral' New Right are women – especially middle-class, middle-aged women. It is clear when we examine the lived experiences of these women why this should be the case. Many of them, albeit willingly, have devoted their lives to their husbands and children (perhaps not realising that an alternative existed). They are aware that they will be judged in their success at being 'good' wives and keeping their husbands happy. They do not want to be seen to have 'failed' in their life's work nor to experience divorce in middle life with no worthwhile skills to sell on the labour market. For many middle-class white women, marriage and domesticity are a rational choice in a patriarchal capitalist society. Working-class women, single parents and black women who could not make this choice and have to struggle to make ends meet, often having to cope with a double shift of domesticity and paid employment or to live in poverty, are also attracted by the image of 'happy families'. Given that society blames parents when things go wrong, it is not surprising that parents presented with portrayals of rising teenage delinquency, sexuality and drug abuse accept the message that this is happening because parental roles have been usurped by professionals – teachers, doctors, and social workers. Women also object to sexual permissiveness and pornography. The Victorian double standard and the sexual exploitation of girls and women by men continue to this day. Women feel objectified by pornography and the ways in which men continually use women to obtain sexual gratification.

In addition, other aspects of New Right ideas appeal to women in other ways. The right-wing idealization of freedom and equality, or getting on through one's own efforts, receives endorsement from middle-class women with aspirations to a career. However, Edwina

Currie, as one example of this type of woman, found that this hypothetical equality did not sufficiently address women's needs. She discovered that she still had to struggle with a patriarchal world in which women were systematically disadvantaged. She says that she has ' ... a growing awareness ... that there is a gap between what women want and what many men who are all for equality and would be horrified to be called sexist believe women want ... (1990, p. 2).

Indeed, Edwina Currie (1990) argues that while the 'moral' New Right's vision of women's role does not appeal to her, neither does the socialist feminist view. However, this perspective also leaves out of account the plight of poorer women who cannot escape into satisfying careers with high economic rewards. As Margaret Thatcher says, *she* could manage a career and motherhood because she had a good nanny. What about the many women who cannot afford a nanny?

The New Right have effectively usurped the moral arguments, by claiming hegemonic status for their views; that is, they claim that there is an absolute morality which their ideas reflect. Others responding to their ideas automatically see 'moral' as having negative resonances and appear to be defending a position of unlimited promiscuity and a rejection of the family. But what is 'moral' about forcing everyone to behave as heterosexuals when some of them are not? What is 'moral' about forcing women to stay in relationships in which they are dependent upon men? What is 'moral' about accepting the poverty of some citizens in the midst of affluence? What is 'moral' about encouraging the pursuit of profit, acquisitiveness and greed at the expense of the most oppressed – and of refusing to take responsibility for less fortunate people as part of the same human community? To us these ideas are immoral. It is necessary to reclaim the 'moral' arguments and to give them a broader social basis.

It is necessary not only to recognise the reasons why the ideas of the moral New Right are attractive to many women as well as men, but to go further and construct a new and coherent morality. Negative criticisms of the New Right leave them in a strong position, because critics frequently appear to be libertarians suggesting that anything goes, that people should have the freedom to seek their own sexual gratification with minimal state regulation. In the economic sphere this is precisely what the Left have rejected, arguing for social justice. However, many men on the left, when it comes to sexuality and other moral issues, do argue for sexual licence. We want to argue for a social morality – social justice in the domestic sphere and in private lives as well as in the public arena.

Feminists have pointed out that arguments for sexual freedom – the case of the sexual liberals – advantage only men. What is being argued for is the right for men to exploit women, and sexuality is a major way in which men do subordinate and exploit women (see Brownmiller, 1976; Jeffreys, 1985; Leidholdt and Raymond, 1990). It is necessary to construct a morality from the position of women – one that does not objectify women and does not permit their sexual exploitation by men. A social morality is one that takes into account the position of the most disadvantaged groups in society. Thus, pornography, prostitution and sexual license are morally wrong because they exploit women.

A social morality needs to be integrated with social justice to provide the ethical basis for society, one that recognises our collective responsibility for all members of our society. A social morality should recognise that when we respect the rights and needs of others, we are acting as moral beings. Socialism and feminism are based upon the idea of collective responsibility, not individualism, and the 'victim-blaming' tendency in individualism is also challenged by collectivism. We recognise that social problems are not caused by individuals but are the outcome of the workings of a patriarchal capitalist society. The construction of this morality enables us to argue for a coherent set of social and moral policies which provide for the needs of all members of our society – men, women and children – whatever family or household organisation they inhabit. As we have argued elsewhere (see Abbott and Wallace 1989), it is necessary to construct social policies on a basis that recognises the different needs of different members of society and of the different members of the family – no matter what form it takes.

Bibliography

Abbott, P. and Wallace, C. (1989) 'The Family' in Brown, P. and Sparks, R. (eds) *Beyond Thatcherism* (Milton Keynes: Open University Press).

Abbott, P. and Wallace, C. (1990a) *An Introduction to Sociology: Feminist Perspectives* (London: Routledge).

Abbott, P. and Wallace, C. (eds) (1990b) *The Sociology of the Caring Professions* (Basingstoke: Falmer).

Abel-Smith, B. and Townsend, P. (1965) *The Poor and the Poorest* (London: Bell).

Achenbaum, W.A. (1986) *Social Security: Visions and Revisions* (Cambridge: Twentieth Century Fund).

Adams, T.K., Duncan, G.J. and Rogers, W.C. (1988) 'The Persistence of Urban Poverty' in Harris, M.F. and Wilkins, R.W. (eds) *Quiet Riots: Race and Poverty in the United States* (New York: Routledge).

Amess, D. (1986) 'Family at the Centre' speech at the launch of the Conservative Family Campaign Press Conference, 14 March, Felixstowe.

Anderson, M. (1964) *The Federal Bulldozer: A Critical Analysis of Urban Renewal 1949–1962* (Cambridge, MA: MIT Press).

Anderson, M. (1978) *Welfare: The Political Economy of Welfare Reforms in the United States* (Stanford, CA: Hoover Institute).

Anderson, M. (1988) *Revolution* (San Diego, CA: Harcourt Brace Jovanovich).

Aries, P. (1965) *Centuries of Childhood: A Social History of Family Life* (New York: Random House).

Bane, M.J. and Jargowsky, P.A. (1988) 'The Links between Government Policy and Family Structure: What Matters and What Doesn't' in Palmer, J.C. and Sawhill, I.V. (eds) *The Changing American Family and Public Policy* (Washington D.C.: Urban Institute Press).

Bawden, L. and Levy, F. (1982) 'The Economic Well-being of Families and Individuals' in Palmer, J.L. and Sawhill, I.V. (eds) *The Reagan Experiment* (Washington D.C.: The Urban Institute Press).

Berger, B. and Berger, P. (1983) *The War Over the Family* (London: Hutchinson).

Bernard, J. (1973) *The Future of Marriage* (London: Souvenir Press).

Beveridge, W. (1942) *Report of the Committee on Social Insurance and Allied Services* (Beveridge Committee) (London: HMSO).

Birke, L. (1980) *Women, Femininity and Biology: The Feminist Challenge* (Sussex: Wheatsheaf).

Block, F., Cloward, R., Ehrenriech, B. and Fox Piven, F. (eds) (1987) *The Mean Season* (New York: Pantheon Books).

Bradshaw, J. and Holmes, H. (1989) *Living on the Edge* (Tyneside: Child Poverty Action Group).

Brimacombe, M. (1987) *Where Homeless Now?* (London: Shelter).

Brown, G.H. and Harris, T.C. (1978) *Social Origins of Depression: a Study of Psychiatric Disorder in Women* (London: Tavistock).

Brownmiller, S. (1976) *Against Our Will: Men, Women and Rape* (Harmondsworth: Penguin).

143

Bruce, S. (1990) *The Rise and Fall of the New Christian Right: Protestant Politics in America 1978–1988* (Oxford: Clarendon Press).

Byrne, D. (1987) 'Rich and Poor: the Growing Divide' in Walker, A. and Walker, C. (eds) *The Growing Divide: A Social Audit 1979–1987* (London: Child Poverty Action Group).

CBPP (Centre on Budget and Policy Priorities) (1988) *Still Far From The Dream: Recent Developments in Black Income, Employment and Poverty* (Washington D.C.: CBPP).

Clarke, J., Cochrane, A. and Smart, C. (1987) *Ideologies of Welfare: from Dreams to Disillusion* (London: Hutchinson).

Conservative Political Centre (1981) *The Future of Marriage* (London: Conservative Central Office).

Committee on Ways and Means, US House of Representatives (1985) *Children in Poverty Appendix C and D* (Washington D.C.: CRO).

Congressional Budget Office (1987) *Work Related Programs for Welfare Recipients* (Washington D.C.: CBO).

Connell, R.M. (1988) 'Opening Statement' in US Congress, Senate Committee on Banking, Housing and Urban Affairs *National Policy Conference and Public Housing* (Washington D.C.: US Government Printing Office).

Conover, P.J. and Gray, V. (1983) *Feminism and the New Right* (New York: Praeger).

Corbett, T. (1985) 'Child Support Assurance: Wisconsin Demonstrations', *Focus*, Spring, pp. 1–5.

Cosmo, G. and Prosser, T. (eds) (1988) *Waiving the Rules: the Constitution under Thatcherism* (Milton Keynes: Open University Press).

Cottingham, P.H. and Ellwood, D.T. (1989) *Welfare Policy for the 1990s* (Cambridge, MA: Harvard University Press).

Cousins, J. and Coote, A. (1981) *The Family in the Firing Line* (London: NCCL/CPAG).

Cox, C. and Boyson, R. (eds) (1977) *Black Papers 1977* (London: Maurice Temple Smith).

Cromartie, C. and Newhaus, R.J. (1987) *Piety and Politics: Evangelical and Fundamentalist Confront the World* (Washington D.C.: Ethics and Public Policy Center).

Currie, E.(ed.) (1990) *What Women Want* (London: Sidgwick and Jackson).

Currie, E. (1990) 'Heavy with Human Tears: Free Market Policy, Inequality and Social Provision in the United States' in Taylor, I. (ed.) *The Social Effects of Free Market Policies: An International Text* (London: Harvester Wheatsheaf).

Currie, E. and Skolnick, J.H. (1988) *America's Problems: Social Issues and Public Policy* 2nd edn. (Glenview, IL: Scott, Foreman).

Danziger, S. and Gottschalk, P. (1985) 'The Poverty of Losing Ground' *Challenge*, May–June, pp. 32–8.

David, M. (1986) 'Morality and Maternity: Towards a Better Union than the Moral Right's Family Policy' *Critical Social Policy*, 61, pp. 40–56.

Davis, L.J. (1980) 'Conservation in America', *Harper's*, vol. 261, pp. 21–6.

Davies, S. (1987) 'Towards the Remoralization of Society' in Loney, M. *et al.* (eds) *The State of the Market* (London: Sage).

Denton, J. (Democrat, Alabama) (1982) Statement to US Congress Senate Committee on Labor and Human Resources, Hearings on 'Work Ethic: Materialism and the American Family' (March).

Department of Health (1990) *Caring for People* (London: HMSO).

Department of Health and Social Security (1985) *Reform of Social Security Vol. 1* (London: HMSO).

Department of Health and Social Security (1988) *Low Income Families 1985* (London: HMSO).

Department of Social Security (1989) *Social Security Statistics* (London: HMSO).

Diamond, S. (1989) *Spiritual Warfare: the Politics of the New Christian Right* (London: Pluto Press).

Digby, A. (1989) *British Welfare Policy: Workhouse to Workfare* (London: Faber and Faber).

Dominelli, L. (1988) 'Thatcher's Attack on Social Security: Restructuring Social Control' *Critical Social Policy*, 23, pp. 46–61.

Edelman, M.W. (1987) *Families in Peril* (Cambridge, MA: Harvard University Press).

Edholm, F. (1982) 'The Unnatural Family' in Whitelegg, E. *et al.* (eds) *The Changing Experience of Women* (Oxford: Martin Robertson).

Ehrenreich, B. (1987) 'The New Right and the Attack on Social Welfare' in Block, F. *et al.* (eds) *The Mean Season*.

Ehrenreich, B. and Fox Piven, F. (1984) 'The Feminisation of Poverty' *Dissent*, Spring, pp. 162–70.

Eisenstein, Z.R. (1984) *Feminism and Sexual Equality* (New York: Monthly Review Press).

Ellwood, D.T. (1988) *Poor Support: Poverty and the American Family* (New York: Basic Books).

Ellwood, D.T. and Bane, M.J. (1984) 'Family Structure and Living Arrangements Research', summary of findings prepared for the US Department of Health and Human Services (March).

Ellwood, D.T. and Summers, L.H. (1986) 'Poverty in America: Is Welfare the Answer or the Problem?' in Danziger, S.H. and Weinberg, D.H. (eds) *Fighting Poverty: What Works and What Doesn't* (Cambridge, MA: Harvard University Press).

Ergas, Y. (1990) 'Madonna and the Politicians: Welfare Reform and the Ambiguities of Policy Making', paper presented at the International Sociological Association Conference, Madrid.

Evans, D. (1989/1990) 'Law, Myth and Paradox' *Critical Social Policy* vol. 9, no. 3 pp. 75–95.

Falwell, J. (1980) *Listen America* (New York: Doubleday).

Foucault, M. (1988) 'Social Security' in Kritzman, L.D. (ed.) *Michel Foucault: Politics, Philosophy and Culture* (London: Routledge).

Fox Piven, F. and Cloward, R.A. (1987) 'The Contemporary Relief Debate' in F. Block *et al.* (eds) *Op. Cit.*

Friedan, B. (1963) *The Feminine Mystique* (New York: Norton).

Gallop G.Jr. (1986) *Gallop Poll: Public Opinion 1985* (Washington D.C.: Scholarly Resources Inc.).

Gamble, A. (1988) *The Free Economy and the Strong State* (London: Macmillan).

Gasper, M. (1981) 'The Dichotomy – Pro-Family/Anti-Family' *The Right Woman*, 5, pp. 57–64.

General Accounting Office (1989) *CWEP's Implementation Results to Date Raise Questions About the Administration's Proposed Mandatory Workfare Program* (Washington: GAO).

Gilder, G. (1973) *Sexual Suicide* (New York: Quadrangle).

Gilder, G. (1974) *Naked Nomads: Unmarried Men in America* (New York: Quadrangle).

Gilder, G. (1978) *Visible Man. A True Story of Post-racist America* (New York: Basic Books).

Gilder, G. (1982) *Wealth and Poverty* (London: Buchan and Enright).

Gilder, G. (1984) 'A vote for My Guy is a Vote for JFK's Legacy' *The Washington Post National Weekly Edition*, vol. 2, no. 2, 12 November, pp. 9–10.

Gilder, G. (1985) *The Spirit of Enterprise* (Harmondsworth: Viking).

Gilder, G. (1986) *Men and Marriage* (Louisiana: Pelican).

Gordon L. and Hunter, A. (1977/1978) 'Sex, Family and the New Right: Anti-feminism as a Political Force' *Radical America*, Vols 11 and 12 (nos 6 and 1, November 1977 and February 1978) pp. 1–7.

Graham, H. (1987) 'Women's Poverty and Earning' in Glendinning, C. and Millar, J. *Women and Poverty in Britain* (Brighton: Wheatsheaf).

Green, D. (1987) *The New Right. The Counter Revolution in Political, Economic and Social Thought* (Sussex: Wheatsheaf).

Green, S., and Webster-Gardiner, G. (1988) *Tax on Marriage* (Manchester: Christians in Britain pamphlet).

Greenstein (1985) 'Losing Faith in Losing Ground' *The New Republic* 192, 25 March, pp. 12–17.

Gregory, J. (1987) *Sex, Race and the Law: Legislating for Equality* (Beverly Hills, LA: Sage).

Hall, S. (1980) *Drifting into a Law and Order Society* (London: Cobden Trust).

Hall, S. (1988) *The Hard Road to Renewal* (London: Verso).

Hall, S. and Jacques, M. (eds) (1983) *The Politics of Thatcherism* (London: Lawrence and Wishart).

Hardy, M. (1990) 'New Times and New Families: Postmodern Society and Lone Parent Families', paper presented at 'Care in the Community' UK/USSR Conference, University of Surrey, June.

Harrington, M. (1962) *The Other America* (New York: Macmillan).

Harrison, B. and Bluestone, B. (1988) *The Great U-Turn: Corporate Restructuring and the Polarising of America* (New York: Basic Books).

Himmelstein, J.L. (1990) *To the Right* (Berkeley, CA: University of California Press).

H.M. Treasury (1988) *The Government Expenditure Plans 1987/8 to 1990/1* (London: HMSO).

Honeyford, R. (1984) 'Education and Race: an Alternative View', *Salisbury Review*, Winter, pp. 30–72.

Jeffreys, S. (1985) *The Spinster and Her Enemies* (London: Pandora).

Jeffreys, S. (1990) *Anticlimax: a Feminist Perspective on Sexual Revolution* (London: The Women's Press).

Jenkins, P. (1977) Speech to Conservative Party Conference.

Jessop, B., Bonnett, K., Bromley, S. and Ling, T. (1988) *Thatcherism* (Oxford: Polity Press).

Johnson, P. (1982) 'Family Reunion' *Observer* 10 October.

Johnson, P. (1987) 'Families under Fire' *Daily Telegraph* 5 January.

Jorstad, E. (1987) *The New Christian Right 1981–1988* (New York: Edwin Mullen Press).

Joseph, K. and Sumption, J. (1979) *Equality* (London: John Murray).

Kammerman, S. and Alfred, K. (1984) 'Income Transfers and Mother Only Families in Eight Countries' *Social Service Review*, September, pp. 448–84.

Kaus, M. (1986) 'The Work Ethic State' *New Republic* 7 July, pp. 22–33.

Kiernan, K. and Wicks, M. (1990) *Family Change and Family Policy* (London: Family Policy Studies Centre).

King, D.S. (1987) *The New Right: Politics, Markets and Citizenship* (London: Macmillan).

Klatch, R.E. (1987) *Women of the New Right* (Philadelphia: Temple University Press).

Krieger, J. (1986) *Reagan, Thatcher and the Politics of Decline* (Cambridge: Polity Press).

Labour Research (1984) 'Pressure Groups: Right Thinking People' vol. 73, no. 2, pp. 37–41.

Labour Research (1985) 'Think Tanks and Pressure Groups' vol. 74, no. 1, pp. 45–8.

Labour Research (1988) 'The Long Claws of the American Right' vol. 77, no. 1, pp. 17–18.

Labour Research (1989) 'Going Right Round the Bend' vol. 78, no. 9, pp. 15–17.

Lasch, C. (1977) *Haven in a Heartless World* (New York: Basic Books).

Leidholdt, D. and Raymond, J.G. (1990) *The Sexual Liberals and the Attack on Feminism* (New York: Pergamon).

Levitan, S. A. and Belous, R.S. (1981) *What's Happening to the American Family?* (Baltimore, MD: Johns Hopkins University Press).

Leys, C. (1990) 'Still a Question of Hegemony' *New Left Review*, 181, pp. 119–27.

Liberman, R.C. (1983) 'Mobilising the Moral Majority' in Hawthorne, M. (ed.) *New Christian Right* (New York: Aldine Books).

London Weekend Edinburgh Return Group (1978) *In and Against the State* (London: Black Rose Press).

Low Pay Unit (1988) 'Poverty: Is the Government Being Statistical with the Truth?' *Low Pay Review*, 34, Summer.

Malpass, P. (1990) 'Housing Policy and the Thatcher Revolution' in Carter, P., Jeffs, T. and Smith, M. (eds) *Social Work and Social Welfare* (Milton Keynes: Open University Press).

Marshall, T.H. (1963) 'Citizenship and Social Class' in Marshall, T.H. *Sociology at the Crossroads* (London: Heinemann).

Martin, J. and Roberts, C. (1984) *Women and Employment: a Life-time Perspective* (London: HMSO).

Mead, L. (1986) *Beyond Entitlement: The Social Obligations of Citizenship* (New York: Free Press).

Millar, J. (1987) 'The Feminisation of Poverty: Lone Mothers and Their Children', paper for CEPS Conference on Demographic Change in Europe and its Socio-Economic Consequences, Belgium.

Miller, D.C. (1990) *Women and Social Welfare: A Feminist Analysis* (New York: Praeger).

Miller, S.M. (1990) 'The New Right and the Re-stratification of the United States', paper presented at International Sociological Association Conference, Madrid, August.

Minford, P. (1989) 'State Expenditure: A Study in Waste' *Economic Affairs* (April–June).

Mishra, R. (1981) *Society and Social Policy* (London: Macmillan).

Morgan, M. (1975) *The Total Woman* (London: Hodder and Stoughton).

Morris, R. (1986) *Rethinking Social Welfare: Why Care for the Scrounger?* (New York: Longman).

Morris, R. (1987) 'Re-thinking Welfare in the United States: the Welfare State in Transition' in Friedman, M.R. and Moshesherer, N.G. (eds) *Modern Welfare States* (Brighton: Wheatsheaf).

Mount, F. (1982) *The Subversive Family* (London: Jonathan Cape).

Moynihan, D.P. (1965) *The Negro Family: The Case for National Action* (Washington D.C.: US Department of Labor/GPO).

Moynihan, D. P. (1986) *Family and Nation* (San Diego: Harcourt Brace Jovanovich).

Murray, C. (1976) *The Link Between Learning Disabilities and Juvenile Delinquency* (US Department of Justice, National Institute for Juvenile Justice and Delinquency Prevention).

Murray, C. (1977) *A Behavioural Study of Modernisation, Social and Economic Change in Thai Villages* (New York: Praeger).

Murray, C. (1984) *Losing Ground. American Social Policy 1950–1980* (New York: Basic Books).

Murray, C. (1988) *In Pursuit of Happiness and Good Government* (New York: Simon and Schuster).

Murray, C. (1990) *The Emerging British Underclass* (London: IEA Health and Welfare Unit, reprinted from *The Sunday Times Magazine* 26 November 1989).

Murray, C. and Cox, L. (1979) *Beyond Probation: Juvenile Corrections and the Chronic Delinquent* (London: Sage).

National Association of Citizens Advice Bureaux (NACAB)(1989) *Income Support and 16–17 Year Olds* (London: NACAB).

National Association of Citizens Advice Bureaux (NACAB) (1990) *Hard Times for Social Fund Applicants* (London: NACAB).

National Rainbow Coalition Health Commission (1988) 'Health is a Human Right: A National Health Program for the United States' *Critical Social Policy*, 22, pp. 80–99.

O'Connor, J. (1977) *Accumulation Crisis* (Oxford: Blackwell).

Pahl, J. (1980) 'Patterns of Money Management within Marriage' *Journal of Social Policy* vol. 9, 3, pp. 313–35.

Paige, C. (1983) *The Right-to-Lifers: Who They Are, How They Operate, Where They Get Their Money* (New York: Summit Books).

Parker, H. (1986) 'Family Income Support: Government Subversion of the Traditional Family' in Anderson, D. (ed.) *Family Portraits* (London: Social Affairs Unit).

Pearson, G. (1983) *Hooligans: A History of Respectable Fears* (London: Macmillan).

Pechman, S (1985) *Who Paid the Taxes 1966–85* (Washington D.C.: Brookings Institute).

Peele, G. (1984) *Revival and Reaction: the Right in Contemporary America* (Oxford: Clarendon Press).

Petchesky, R.P. (1984) *Abortion and Women's Choice* (New York: Longman).

Pheonix, A. (1990) *Young Mothers* (London: Macmillan).

Raison, T. (1990) *Tories and the Welfare State: A History of Conservative Social Policy since the Second World War* (London: Macmillan).

Randall, G. (1989) *Homeless and Hungry* (London: Centrepoint Soho).

Reagan, R. (1980) 'Acceptance Speech, Republican Presidential Nomination at Detroit', quoted in Morris, R. (1986) *Rethinking Social Welfare* pp. 24–5.

Reimer, B.R. (1988) *The Prisoners of Welfare: Liberating America's Poor from Unemployment and Low Wages* (New York: Praeger).

Rodgers, H.R. (1986) *Poor Women, Poor Families: The Economic Plight of American Female-headed Households* (Armont: M.E. Sharpe).

Rogers, A. and Clements, B. (1985) *The Moral Basis of Freedom* (Exeter: Victoria Books).

Rose, N. (1985) *The Psychological Complex. Psychology, Politics and Society in England 1869–1939* (London: Routledge and Kegan Paul).

Rustin, M. (1985) *For a Pluralist Socialism* (London: Verso).

Sandejur D. (1988) 'Blacks, Hispanics, American Indians and Poverty – and What Worked' in Harris, M.F. and Wilkins, R.W. (eds) *Quiet Riots: Race and Poverty in the United States* (New York: Routledge).

Segalman, R. and Marsland, D. (1989) *Cradle to Grave: Comparative Perspectives on the Study of Welfare* (London: Macmillan in association with the Social Affairs Unit).

Scruton, R. (ed.)(1984) *The Meaning of Conservatism* 2nd edn. (London: Macmillan).

Scruton, R. (1986) *Sexual Desire* (London: Weidenfeld and Nicolson).

Seebohm Committee (1968) *Report of the Committee on Local Authority and Allied Personal Social Service* (London: HMSO).

Shorter, E. (1975) *The Making of the Modern Family* (Glasgow: Collins).

Smart, C. (1984) *The Ties that Bind* (London: Routledge and Kegan Paul).

Smart, C. (1987) 'Securing the family? Rhetoric and Policy in the Field of Social Security' in Loney, M. (ed.) *The State or the Market* (London: Sage).

Social Services Committee (1986) *Public Expenditure on Social Services* (London: HMSO).

Squires, P. (1990) *Anti-Social Policy: Welfare, Ideology and the Disciplinary State* (Brighton: Harvester Wheatsheaf).

Stack, C. (1974) *All Our Kin: Strategies for Survival in a Black Community* (New York: Harper and Row).

Steadman Jones, G. (1971) *Outcast London: A Study in the Relationship between Classes in Victorian Society* (London: Open University Press).

Steiner, G. (1981) *The Futility of Family Policy* (Washington D.C.: Brookings Institute).

Stockman, D.K. (1986) *The Triumph of Politics* (London: Bodley Head).

Stone, L. (1977) *The Family, Sex and Marriage in England 1500–1800* (London: Weidenfeld and Nicolson).

Summers, Y. (1991) 'Women and Citizenship: the Insane, the Insolvent and the Inanimate?' in Abbott, P. and Wallace, C. (eds) *Women, Power and Sexuality* (London: Macmillan).

Taylor, I. (ed.) (1990) *The Social Effects of Free Market Policies* (London: Harvester Wheatsheaf).

Tebbit, N. (1985) *The Values of Freedom* (London: Conservative Political Centre).

ten Tucsher, T. (1986) 'Feminist Perspectives on the New Right' in Evans, J. *et al.* (eds) *Feminism and Political Theory* (London: Sage).

Thatcher, M. (1977) *Let our Children Grow Tall* (London: Centre for Policy Studies).

Townsend, P. (1979) *Poverty in the United Kingdom* (Harmondsworth: Penguin).

Townsend, P. (1983) 'A Theory of Poverty and the Role of Social Policy' in Loney, M., Boswell, D. and Clarke, J. *Social Policy and Social Welfare* (Milton Keynes: Open University Press).

Tracey, M. and Morrison, D. (1979) *Whitehouse* (London: Macmillan).

US Congress (1985) *The Congressional Record in the Hatch Coalition and American Educational Research Association. The Hatch Ammendment Regulations* (Washington D.C: AERA).

US Congress (1988) *Children and Families: Key Trends in the 1980's. House Select Committee on Children, Youth and Families* (Washington D.C.: US Government Printing Office).

Viguerie, R. (1981) *The New Right: We're Ready to Lead* (Fall Church: Viguerie).

Walby, S. (1990) *Theorizing Patriarchy* (Oxford: Blackwell).

Wallace, C. (1987) *For Richer, For Poorer* (London: Tavistock).

Watts, R. (1990) 'Jam Every Other Day: Living Standards and the Hawke Government 1983–1989' in Taylor, I. (ed.) *The Social Effects of free Market Policies*.

Webster-Gardiner, G. (1986) 'Putting Father Back at the Head of the Table', speech at press conference launch of Conservative Family Campaign, 14 March, Felixstowe.

Weir, M., Orlaff, A.S. and Skocpol, T. (1988) *The Politics of Social Policy in the United States* (Princeton, NJ: Princeton University Press).

Weyrich, P. (1983) 'Family Issues' in Phillips, H. (ed.) *The New Right at Harvard* (Vienna, VA: The Conservative Caucus, Inc.).

Williams, F. (1989) *Social Policy: a Critical Introduction* (Cambridge: Polity).

Wilson, E. (1977) *Women and the Welfare State* (London: Tavistock).

Wilson, W.J. and Neckerman, R.M. (1986) 'Poverty and Family Structure: the Widening Gap between Evidence and Public Policy Issues' in Danziger, S.H. and Weinberg, D.H. (eds) *Fighting Poverty: What Works and What Doesn't* (Cambridge, MA: Harvard University Press).

Worsthorne, P. (1986) 'Why charity is the Best Hope for the Poor' *Sunday Telegraph* 21 December.

Wright, G. (ed.) (1989) *The ABC of Thatcherism* (London: Fabian Society).

Name Index

Subject Index